The Object Le_____se
to magic: the b_____ objects
and animate the___ ____ a rich history of invention,
political struggle, science, and popular mythology. Filled
with fascinating details and conveyed in sharp, accessible
prose, the books make the everyday world come to life.
Be warned: once you've read a few of these, you'll start
walking around your house, picking up random objects,
and musing aloud: 'I wonder what the story is behind
this thing?'"

Steven Johnson, author of *Where Good Ideas*
Come From and *How We Got to Now*

In 1957 the French critic and semiotician Roland
Barthes published *Mythologies*, a groundbreaking series
of essays in which he analysed the popular culture of
his day, from laundry detergent to the face of Greta
Garbo, professional wrestling to the Citroën DS. This
series of short books, Object Lessons, continues the
tradition."

Melissa Harrison, *Financial Times*

Though short, at roughly 25,000 words apiece, these
books are anything but slight."

Marina Benjamin, *New Statesman*

The joy of the series, of reading *Remote Control, Golf Ball, Driver's License, Drone, Silence, Glass, Refrigerator, Hotel,* and *Waste* (more titles are listed as forthcoming) in quick succession, lies in encountering the various turns through which each of their authors has been put by his or her object. As for Benjamin, so for the authors of the series, the object predominates, sits squarely center stage, directs the action. The object decides the genre, the chronology, and the limits of the study. Accordingly, the author has to take her cue from the *thing* she chose or that chose her. The result is a wonderfully uneven series of books, each one a *thing* unto itself."

Julian Yates, *Los Angeles Review of Books*

The Object Lessons project, edited by game theory legend Ian Bogost and cultural studies academic Christopher Schaberg, commissions short essays and small, beautiful books about everyday objects from shipping containers to toast. *The Atlantic* hosts a collection of "mini object-lessons"… More substantive is Bloomsbury's collection of small, gorgeously designed books that delve into their subjects in much more depth."

Cory Doctorow, *Boing Boing*

OBJECT LESSONS

A book series about the hidden lives of ordinary things.

Series Editors:

Ian Bogost and Christopher Schaberg

Advisory Board:

Sara Ahmed, Jane Bennett, Jeffrey Jerome Cohen, Johanna Drucker, Raiford Guins, Graham Harman, renée hoogland, Pam Houston, Eileen Joy, Douglas Kahn, Daniel Miller, Esther Milne, Timothy Morton, Kathleen Stewart, Nigel Thrift, Rob Walker, Michele White.

In association with

BOOKS IN THE SERIES

questionnaire

EVAN KINDLEY

Bloomsbury Academic
An imprint of Bloomsbury Publishing Inc

B L O O M S B U R Y
NEW YORK · LONDON · OXFORD · NEW DELHI · SYDNEY

Bloomsbury Academic
An imprint of Bloomsbury Publishing Inc

1385 Broadway
New York
NY 10018
USA

50 Bedford Square
London
WC1B 3DP
UK

www.bloomsbury.com

BLOOMSBURY and the Diana logo are trademarks of Bloomsbury Publishing Plc

First published 2016

Library of Congress Cataloging-in-Publication Data
Names: Kindley, Evan, author.
Title: Questionnaire / Evan Kindley.
Description: New York : Bloomsbury Academic, [2016] | Series: Object lessons | Includes bibliographical references and index.
Identifiers: LCCN 2015050479 (print) | LCCN 2016008073 (ebook) | ISBN 9781501314773 (paperback) | ISBN 9781501314797 (ePub) | ISBN 9781501314780 (ePDF)
Subjects: LCSH: Questionnaires—History. | Questionnaires—Methodology. | Social surveys—History. | BISAC: LITERARY CRITICISM / Semiotics & Theory. | PHILOSOPHY / Aesthetics. | SOCIAL SCIENCE / Media Studies.
Classification: LCC HM537 .K56 2016 (print) | LCC HM537 (ebook) | DDC 300.72/3—dc23
LC record available at http://lccn.loc.gov/2015050479

ISBN: PB: 978-1-5013-1477-3
ePub: 978-1-5013-1479-7
ePDF: 978-1-5013-1478-0

Series: Object Lessons

Cover design: Alice Marwick
Cover image © Alice Marwick

Typeset by Deanta Global Publishing Services, Chennai, India
Printed and bound in the United States of America

To Emily, for everything,
but especially _____

I am beginning to wonder
Whether this alternative to
Sitting back and doing something quiet
Is the clever initiative it seemed.
                    —John Ashbery, "Proust's Questionnaire"

CONTENTS

INTRODUCTION: THE FORM AS FORM

Why do people like to fill out questionnaires? Well, first of all: *do* they? Many questionnaires, maybe most, are no fun to fill out at all. We complete them only reluctantly, at the DMV and the doctor's office, during tax season or to file insurance claims, when pollsters call or corner us, or in order to purchase goods, qualify for coupons, or view online content. In such everyday moments of confrontation with questionnaires, we are rarely enjoying ourselves; sometimes, it's all we can do to check our exasperation.

But then there are the *other* types of questionnaires: personality tests; dating profiles; online quizzes—we like those. Indeed, it would not be exaggerating much to say we love them. Copyrighted psychological tests like the Myers-Briggs Type Indicator (MBTI), the Revised NEO Personality Inventory, and the Enneagram bring in millions of dollars every year for their publishers. The Internet's most popular dating site, Match.com, has 2.39 million subscribers, and most of what they do is respond to questionnaires. BuzzFeed's highest-charting quiz, "What State Do You Actually Belong In?," had over 42 million page views as of December 2015.[1] No one is forcing anyone to answer any of these questions. The fact must be faced: for many of us, under the right circumstances, filling out forms is fun.

It took centuries for this idea of fun to develop, however. Most premodern questionnaires, like the "cédula" issued in 1577 by King Philip II of Spain to account for royal holdings in the Indies, were instruments of governance geared toward enumerating and keeping track of state property; they were not beloved. The word "questionnaire" appears first in French, in its modern sense, in the mid-nineteenth century. Some of the word's early usages suggest persistent associations with the Catholic practices of catechism and confession, as well as governmental inquisition and interrogation. (In the eighteenth century, the term "questionnaire-juré" described a torturer.)

Questionnaires weren't instruments of torture, exactly, but they *were* vehicles of the scarcely more popular process of taxation. Respondents were asked about things that could easily be identified, described, and counted, and in which the state might take an interest: primarily money and property. It was not always easy to get people to respond. Hostility toward taxation seems to have bled into people's reactions to other kinds of surveys as well. In the late seventeenth and early eighteenth centuries, naturalists inspired by Sir Francis Bacon experimented with questionnaires as a means for soliciting reports about the flora and fauna of distant regions to which it would be impracticable to travel. From 1645 on, a group of "intelligencers" associated with the agricultural reformer Samuel Hartlib issued a series of surveys to landed gentry and parish priests about the features of their respective home regions. The first entry of Thomas Machell's snappily titled *That the northern counties which abound in antiquities and ancient gentry, may no longer be bury'd in silence information is desir'd concerning the following queries as they lye in order*, for instance, reads: "1. The name of the Parish, & why so call'd? how written in ancient Records? In what Diocese, Barony, Hundred or Ward is it said to lye? How is it bounded & divided from other Parishes on the E, W, N, & South &c? by what Rivers, Hedges, Walls, Cause-ways, or common and well known Land-markes, Meets and Boundaries &c, or are they (or any of them) Litigious or Doubtfull?"

All of these early scientific questionnaires had return rates approaching zero. When they came back at all, the respondents often expressed skepticism toward the entire enterprise. One landowner wrote that he did not care "to be concerned over much in any business that has not (at least) some appearance either of present pleasure or future profit." "What is surprising, perhaps, is not that the returns to such inquiries were so poor," the historian Adam Fox observes, "but that researchers continued to be optimistic about their value for so long."[2] Fox is right: it's remarkable that, in the face of overwhelming indifference, scholars persevered in crafting elaborate prompts and instructions for no one, sending out inquiry after inquiry into the abyss. Faith in the potential value of the questionnaire was strong enough to overcome its present uselessness. Throughout the eighteenth and even into the nineteenth century, the questionnaire was less a viable research technique than a utopian literary genre, linked to an idea of the scientific perfection of society. A better world could be realized, reformers dreamed—or at least some progress toward it could be made—if we could simply get people to fill out the necessary forms.

*

Questionnaires are a species within a larger genus, which is the blank form. In her book *Paper Knowledge*, the media scholar Lisa Gitelman emphasizes the importance of blank "job-printed" forms to the rise of bureaucracy and the consolidation of the new capitalist economy in the nineteenth and twentieth centuries.[3] Blank forms, Gitelman argues, are the ultimate bureaucratic objects: bland, impersonal, utilitarian documents designed to help officials process and sort large groups of people.

The history of the questionnaire is the history of attempts to make interacting with such dreary objects more and more fun for more and more people. Tactics have changed considerably over the years, to be sure. Statesmen and scientists began by thinking of personal questions as something their subjects would only tolerate under compulsion, but as time passed it became clearer that people can actually *enjoy* interrogation by questionnaire, to the point where they will actively seek out the experience. The history of the questionnaire is thus also a history of psychological manipulation, and of salesmanship: a series of attempts to find the magic words that will open the heart of the public.

In 2016 we fill out more questionnaires than ever, although we're far less likely to write out our responses by hand or speak them to another human being than type them into a computer or tap them out on a smartphone. When you sign up for a social media service like Facebook, you fill out a form with your basic vitae: your name, your age, where you live, where you work, and so on, for however long you feel like going. *How do you pronounce your name? What are your favorite quotations? What movies and books and musical artists do you like?* When you purchase products from Amazon or any other online retailer, you fill out a form with your address, your credit card information, your preferred shipping method. If you want to help their algorithms get better at recommending things, you can answer more queries about the types of products you prefer. When you join a dating service like Match.com, eHarmony, or OkCupid, the first thing you do is answer a series of personal questions designed to help pinpoint your perfect match. The services work better the more questions you answer. When you're tired of work and need a break, you head over to BuzzFeed and take a quiz. You answer questions. The quiz tells you what you are. You post it to Facebook. Other people tell you what they are, too.

Why are we answering all these questions? What is the appeal of the questionnaire? How has it become so omnipresent in our lives? The seven chapters that follow will trace the development of the personal questionnaire, from its sudden prominence in Victorian Britain to its current ubiquity on the social Web. To follow the questionnaire through time requires detours through the history of science as well as the history of popular culture. It is an unusual object in that it has been batted like a tennis ball between the realms of experimental science and the mass media, rarely coming to rest in one sector for long, but picking up spin and momentum from each volley. In the 1870s, questionnaires were used simultaneously by statisticians to gather anthropometric data and as parlor games to amuse the English bourgeoisie. In the early twentieth century they were adopted by organizational psychologists and refashioned into tools of evaluation and assessment. In the 1960s and 1970s, they lost most of their scientific prestige but became popular with a wider audience than ever, thanks to their dissemination via mass-market women's magazines like *Cosmopolitan*. Finally, in the twenty-first century, questionnaires have once again become instruments of data collection for the purposes of statistical analysis, albeit now on a vaster scale than their original pioneers could have imagined.

Over the course of this messy, discontinuous history, personal questionnaires have been put to many different uses, not all of them respectable or even ethical, and the willingness of the public to submit to them has waxed and waned (but mostly waxed). The first recipients of questionnaires found them confounding, confusing, frightening, and unwelcome.

They looked like instruments of torture or the inquiries of government spies. As the forms became more familiar, we forgot our early suspicions, and learned to stop worrying and love the questionnaire.

We may now be experiencing a pendulum swing in the other direction. In the last few years, thanks to recent revelations about the extent of state surveillance and public arguments about the rise of Big Data in a variety of cultural fields, the compilation of personal information has become a vital political issue. But even as these developments have stoked our paranoia and our cynicism, our browsing habits have hardly changed. Today we are both more suspicious and more careless than our seventeenth-century forebears. Our attitudes toward the mass collection of personal data veer wildly, day to day, from avidity to anger to resignation and back again. We know that "they" are watching us and we are outraged and we don't care. In this strange climate, it's worth recalling that the decision to provide information about oneself, as irresistible as it sometimes seems, is neither a natural human instinct nor an automatic social good.

So what is it, then?

Good question.

1 PRIVATE PUBLICITY

In 1870, an English scientist named Francis Galton submitted a seven-page questionnaire to 180 members of the Royal Society of London for Improving Natural Knowledge. Though hardly lacking in ambition, Galton was not at all confident of his success. "It was a daring undertaking, to ask as I did, in 1874, every Fellow of the Royal Society who had filled some important post, to answer a multitude of Questions needful for my purpose, a few of which touched on religion and other delicate matters," he recalled in his 1908 autobiography. "The size of my circular was alarming. . . . Much experience of sending circular questions has convinced me of the impossibility of foretelling whether a particular person will receive them kindly or not. Some are unexpectedly touchy." One "man of high scientific distinction," Galton remembered, "was almost furious at being questioned. On the other hand, a Cabinet Minister, whom I knew but slightly, gave me full and very interesting information without demur."[1]

Galton's nervousness about his "daring undertaking" is not surprising. Many of his queries, even by today's standards, are invasive. They touch on ancestry ("Your father and mother, are they respectively English, Welsh, Scotch, Irish, Jewish, or foreign?"), physical characteristics ("Temperament, if distinctly nervous, sanguine, bilious, or lymphatic? Measurement round inside rim of your hat?"), education ("How long were you at small schools, large schools, universities, and what ages?"), and matters of belief ("Has the religion taught in your youth had any deterrent effect on the freedom of your researches?"), among other sensitive topics. Galton felt the need to reassure the respondents that the responses would be kept anonymous. "Entries marked 'Private' will be dealt with *in strict confidence*," he assured the questionnaire's recipients; "they will be used only as data for general statistical conclusions."[2]

Galton's survey was ultimately answered by about a hundred scientists—including Charles Darwin and James Clerk Maxwell—and the results were eventually published (anonymously) and analyzed in Galton's 1874 volume *English Men of Science: Their Nature and Nurture*. The immediate aim of the book was to refute the arguments of the Swiss botanist Augustin Pyramus de Candolle, who held that environment, and not genetic predisposition, was the determining factor in scientific achievement. But Galton didn't stop there. From his data, he drew a raft of dubious generalizations. He concluded, for instance, that "the character of scientific men is strongly anti-feminine. Their mind is directed to facts and abstract theories, and not to persons or human interests. . . . In many respects they have little sympathy with female ways of thought."[3] He also found that men of science were hostile toward classical education and religion: all opinions that dovetailed, as it happened, with Galton's own.

Whatever the merits of his scientific conclusions—which, even at the time, were met with skepticism—Galton's study was a definite methodological success. More than any other single scientific work, *English Men of Science* established the self-report questionnaire in the United Kingdom as a legitimate instrument for the collection of empirical data. A few years later, in 1879, Galton solidified his status as a founding father of questionnaire research by drafting a document called "Questions on visualising and other allied faculties." Known as the "breakfast table questionnaire" because it asked respondents to describe the appearance of their morning repast, the exercise was a landmark in experimental psychology; a version of it is still used by clinicians to test visual imaging capacity today.

After these preliminary successes, much of Galton's energy would go toward convincing his contemporaries to respond to more and more questionnaires. Historically, this had been a Herculean task, as the Hartlib circle's poor response rates attest. Galton, an ardent social reformer as well as a scientist, shared his predecessors' ambition and idealism: he, too, imagined a world remade by asking the right questions. But the specific details of his utopianism now seem more than a little disturbing. Like many of his contemporaries, Galton held deeply racist beliefs, which in his case had been reinforced by visits to Africa and the Middle East in the 1840s and 1850s. The superiority of white Europeans to all other races was, for him, an article of faith. Both *Hereditary Genius* and *English Men of Science* laid the foundation for eugenics, a science Galton both named and pioneered. In a paper published in the *American Journal of Sociology* in 1904, Galton defined it as "the science which deals with all influences that improve the inborn qualities of a race; also with those that develop them to the utmost advantage."[4]

In simultaneously fostering the sciences of anthropometrics, statistics, and evolutionary biology, Galton sought to create a discipline that would be able to not only understand human reproduction but, more important, control it. Eugenics, once perfected, would produce an "exact stocktaking of the nation" that would in turn allow the state to identify individuals who were "hereditarily remarkable" and encourage them to breed with one another.[5] Their genetic inferiors, meanwhile—most of whom were to be found among the lower classes and non-white races— would be discouraged from reproducing at all. (What form this discouragement would take was a little vague. Unlike many of his followers, Galton never advocated for forced sterilization, though he did, in his unpublished utopian novel *Kantsaywhere*, imagine state-run labor camps for "the naturally feeble.")[6]

The eugenics movement would go on to have a catastrophic influence in the first half of the twentieth century, most notably in Nazi Germany, and there is no question that Galton (though he died in 1911, before eugenics' worst excesses would become evident) deserves a share of the shame. For the moment, however, I am less concerned with *what* Galton was trying to prove—the genetic superiority of white European aristocrats to all other human beings on the planet—than with *how* he went about proving it. In his work on heredity, he took the first steps toward solving a major practical problem for the social sciences: how to convince people to overcome their disinclination to provide personal information about themselves. "Most men and women shrink from having their hereditary worth recorded," Galton observed in the *Fortnightly Review* in 1883. "There may be family diseases of which they hardly dare to speak, except on rare occasions and then in whispered hints or obscure phrases, as though timidity of utterance could hush thoughts, and as though what they fondly suppose to be locked-up domestic secrets may not be bruited about with exaggeration among the surrounding gossips." This reluctance to share accurate details of family medical history seemed to Galton "ignoble," and yet, "moralise as we may, the difficulty remains."

The solution, he decided, was to target "medical men" specifically, who he believed would "be tempted, by an appeal to their scientific zeal . . . to write about themselves, at their best, and in great multitudes." At the same time, he exploited financial instincts, offering cash prizes of up to £500 to "those candidates who shall best succeed in defining vividly, completely, and concisely the characteristics (medical and other) of the various members of their respective families, and in illustrating the presence or absence of hereditary influences."

Finally, he appealed to Victorian domestic sentiment, claiming that the completion of his questionnaires would bring families closer together. "The inquiries I wish to set in motion by means of these prizes are undertakings in which many relatives will gladly join," he predicted. "It involves much pleasant correspondence with early friends who had long dropped out of sight, and it creates an agreeable bond of interest with relations living at a distance." The emphasis was on the generation of family heirlooms rather than of experimental data. "Whatever may be the value of these results, the facts incidentally obtained during the course of the inquiry will form a separate document much prized by the family," Galton declared, and he collaborated with the publishing industry to produce such documents.[7] In 1884 Macmillan brought out *Record of Family Faculties*, and supplemented it with a pamphlet entitled the *Life History Album*, in which new or expectant parents could record the development of their offspring as they grew. With this stratagem, Galton invented the baby book, a popular genre that continues to flourish today.

*

Why did scientific questionnaires catch on when they did, after so many decades of failure? Why were the Victorians more eager to answer questions about themselves than any previous generation of British subjects? Family values, financial incentives, and professional obligations all played a role, as did literacy rates, which had risen dramatically since

Hartlib's time, greatly increasing the potential audience for printed questionnaires of any kind. But there was also an important shift in public sensibility. Where the landed gentry of the seventeenth and eighteenth centuries were suspicious of detailed requests for information, associating such probes with taxation and unwelcome government interference, the Victorian middle classes felt flattered by the attentions of scientists, and were surprisingly eager to cooperate with them. Galton's Anthropometric Laboratory at the London International Health Exhibition in 1884 attracted crowds of visitors clamoring to be interrogated and measured, including Prime Minister William Ewart Gladstone.

A combination of rationalism, progressivism, and narcissism drove the early development of the questionnaire. The Victorians loved questionnaires because they pandered to their faith in science, their earnest desire to improve the world around them, and—most important, perhaps—their intense interest in the quotidian details of their own lives. Indeed, the mania for anthropometric questionnaires bears a curious similarity to another contemporary trend among the British middle class of the late nineteenth century: the vogue for confession albums, which were a popular parlor game in the 1870s and later. The confession album was a Victorian variation on the medieval *album amicorum* or *stammbuch* ("friendship book") in which one collected the autographs of one's bosom companions. In the confession album, however, one asked friends to record not only their names but also their answers to questions such as "What do you consider the most beautiful thing in nature?" and "What peculiarity can you most tolerate?" The word "confession" implies secrecy, but it is clear from surviving albums, which often contain responses by multiple hands, that they were freely and frequently passed around among groups of friends. Like the personal details that circulate on today's social media, these revelations were not true confessions but symbolic tokens meant to be shared. They functioned as a kind of intimate currency among the literate classes.

Confession albums were primarily marketed toward women, and it appears that they were often used as props in courtship rituals, to facilitate conversation and flirting between the sexes. Some sample questions from *The Querist's Album*, from 1878, give a sense of how this may have worked:

What is your opinion of the girl of the period?

What is your opinion of the young man of the period?

At what age should a man marry?

At what age should a woman marry?

Should it be the ladies' prerogative to pop the question?

Do you believe in love at first sight?

Do you believe in marrying for love and working for money?

Were you ever in love? and if so, how often?

What colored eyes and hair do you most admire?

One can imagine any of these delicate queries giving rise to some glittering table talk, or even a tête-à-tête between a hostess and a potential suitor that might lead—who knows?—to a marriage proposal. But "while men and women participated equally in confession albums," the scholar Samantha Matthews writes, "[i]t appears that women may have taken them more seriously. . . . Where men participated they did so at the behest of women, to whom such revelations appeared more significant." She notes the marked difference in tone between male and female responses: while women usually answered sincerely, men often treated the exercise with a mix of condescension and outright contempt. For instance, one "Arthur R.C. Jones" answers that the "noblest aim in life" is "to make money," and that his favorite flowers are nettles.[8]

This cynical masculine attitude is encapsulated by Aubrey Beardsley's "The Story of a Confession-Album," which appeared in the magazine *Tit Bits* in 1889. "Of all the minor nuisances of life, I think none surpass the Confession Album," Beardsley's male narrator complains:

> It is a miserable sort of private publicity, a new inquisition, though no doubt it is as well-meant as the old one. . . . I know not which is the more trying ordeal; to write your own "confession" or to read those of other people. The general opinion appears to be that it is very funny to make yourself out as fast or as foolish as possible; though even worse than this is the painful orthodoxy of those

individuals who claim Shakespeare for their favourite poet, Beethoven for their favourite composer, and Raphael for their favourite painter.[9]

Despite the mixed reputation of this "new inquisition" among gentlemen, many prominent nineteenth-century intellectuals submitted to it. Among them were Karl Marx (who considered his chief characteristic "singleness of purpose" and whose favorite occupation was "bookworming"), Friedrich Engels (whose idea of misery was "to go to a dentist"), Oscar Wilde (who wrote that his distinguishing characteristic was "inordinate self-esteem" and that his bête noire was "a thorough Irish Protestant"), and Arthur Conan Doyle (who refused to answer several questions and described his present state of mind as "jaded"). Journalists, especially in France, helped to publicize these celebrity confessions. In 1892, the magazine *La Revue illustrée* sent a confession-album-like questionnaire to a group of famous writers, including Émile Zola, and printed their responses over the course of several months under the title "Les confidences du salon."[10]

Most of these literary confessions are curios of their era, remembered only by historians and literary scholars. One of them, though, has managed to transcend its original context and continues to have a surprising influence. In 1886, at the tender age of thirteen, Marcel Proust filled out a page in an English confession album belonging to his childhood friend Antoinette Faure (the daughter of future French President Félix Faure). The questionnaire's hallowed reputation is attributable in part to the fact that the young Marcel gave such precociously Proustian answers. To the prompt "Your favorite virtue?" he replied "All those that are not specific to any one sect; the universal ones." The rather pedestrian question "Where would you like to live?" inspired a little burst of metaphysical enthusiasm: "In the realm of the ideal, or rather my ideal." His "idea of misery," true to form, was "to be separated from Maman." And when asked, "For what fault have you most toleration?" he replied "For the private lives of geniuses."

In 1891, at the age of twenty, Proust completed a second (slightly less memorable) questionnaire; this one was actually published during his lifetime in *La Revue illustrée*, under the title "Salon Confidences written by Marcel." The 1886 confession, however, was only discovered and published in 1924, shortly after the author's death, by Antoinette Faure's son, the psychoanalyst André Berge. In an article titled "About a Lucky Find" in the literary journal *Les Cahiers du mois*, Berge described coming across his mother's old confession album in a "heap of volumes transformed by humidity into a kind of sticky paste that formed a bond between the few pitiful survivors." Alongside a reproduction of the questionnaire itself, Berge offered a subtle psychoanalytic *explication de texte*, noting, for instance, that for the "idea of misery" question Proust had first written "to be away from Mother" and then crossed it out and replaced "to be away" with "to be separated." "With this cross-out," Berge theorized, "we can surely recognize the everlasting unease of the great psychologist who, in his subtle turns of phrase, strived to reflect the most elusive nuances of thought no matter what."

Berge's text inaugurates the fetishism of what would soon become known far and wide as "le questionnaire de Proust." Interestingly, he denigrates the confession album's "stupid questions" while praising Proust's ingenious answers.[11] But in fairly short order the questions themselves began to take on a totemic significance, first for writers and literary scholars and, subsequently, for the culture at large. For a couple of scraps of literary juvenilia, the two questionnaires answered by Proust have had a truly remarkable afterlife. High school teachers give them to their students to help them write more revealing recommendations; novelists and screenwriters fill them out on behalf of their characters to make them more "well-rounded." The documents themselves have taken on the status of holy relics: in 2003, the manuscript of the 1886 Proust questionnaire was sold at auction for 102,000 euros (equivalent to $120,000).[12]

How did this alchemy take place? For a few decades, the "questionnaire de Proust" was known mainly to literary scholars and certain denizens of the European avant-garde. By the 1950s and 1960s, however, versions of the questionnaire had begun to appear regularly in upmarket French magazines like *Biblio*, *L'Express*, and *Le Point*, eventually becoming a staple of European middlebrow journalism. The German newspaper *Frankfurter Allgemeine Zeitung* adopted a version of the Proust questionnaire in the 1980s, as did the English *Sunday Correspondent* magazine, on the advice of the novelist

Gilbert Adair, who noted shrewdly that "the advantage of questionnaires, from a financial point of view, was that not one of the celebrities who agree to submit [answers] expect to be paid."[13]

In 1993, *Vanity Fair*, under the editorship of Graydon Carter, started running a regular "Proust Questionnaire" feature on its back page, thus bringing the format to a mass American audience for the first time. Respondents were not limited to the usual authors and intellectuals (though Norman Mailer, Fran Lebowitz, Joan Didion, and many other writers did participate) but extended to celebrity chefs like Julia Child, fashion designers like Karl Lagerfeld, and movie stars like Arnold Schwarzenegger. (The latter's answer to the "lowest depths of misery" question: "Did you read the reviews for *Last Action Hero*?") In 2009, the magazine published an anthology of these questionnaires and, to promote it, launched "Turbo Proust!," an interactive online version of the Proust questionnaire, which allows you to submit to the questions yourself and compare your answers to those of luminaries from the *Vanity Fair* archives. (A Flash-animated likeness of Marcel in the upper left corner blinks and wiggles his mustache at you as you do so.)[14]

It is television, though, that has been the most effective popularizer of the Proust questionnaire. In 1975, the French talk show host Bernard Pivot adopted a version of it as the signature closing segment of his literary panel show *Apostrophes*. In fact, though he invariably presented it as an homage to the author, Pivot's list of ten questions—including

"What is your favorite curse word?" and "If God exists, what would you like to hear him say to you after your death?"—didn't share a single item in common with the questionnaire answered by Proust. *Apostrophes* was astonishingly popular in France—at its height, it reached an audience of 6.4 million—and the questionnaire featured in every episode, where it was answered by the likes of Susan Sontag and Alexander Solzhenitsyn. James Lipton, the man who would bring Pivot's version of the Proust questionnaire to America, first saw it on the TV network of the City University of New York in the 1980s. "I had surfed past the channel," Lipton remembers in his 2007 autobiography; "then, spying a portrait of Rimbaud in a show's opening titles, doubled back to look again at an unaccustomed sight: several people seated in a semicircle, facing a professorial personage surrounded by books bristling with bookmarks." Though impressed by the sophistication of the program overall, Lipton was entranced by the questionnaire feature in particular: "Toward the end of the broadcast," he writes, "the host unfurled a list of questions unlike any I'd ever heard before: a kind of verbal Rorschach test that told the viewer more about the respondent in a one-word answer than an hour of questioning might have revealed."[15] Lipton subsequently borrowed the device for his own show *Inside the Actor's Studio*, which began airing on the cable network Bravo in 1994. *Apostrophes* had gone off the air in 1989, but Pivot's next series *Bouillon de culture* also incorporated the questionnaire; on the show's final broadcast in 2001, Pivot and Lipton submitted to it themselves, for the first time, in tandem.

In all of these contexts, being asked to respond to the so-called "Proust questionnaire" is presented as a kind of high honor, a way of signaling that you and your body of work stand above the humdrum promotional cycle. You are there to do more than hawk a product; the audience is interested, above all, in *you*. Whereas the Victorian confession album had frankly sought to orient its respondents toward contemporary life ("What is your opinion of the young man of the period?"), the latter-day Proust questionnaire is intended to grant the tastes, opinions, and preferences of celebrities a timeless philosophical interest. Unlike the typical journalistic interview, the questions that make up the Proust questionnaire are not specifically matched to the respondent, and the standardization of the exercise somehow forms part of its prestige. Whether you're a philosopher or a sitcom actor, the questions are the same. It is your answers—and the fact that you've been asked at all—that affirms your specialness.

What would Proust have thought of the "Proust questionnaire" phenomenon? It seems likely that he would have despised it. In his unfinished critical work *Contre Sainte-Beuve*, he railed against biographical interest in the personal lives of writers. He firmly opposed the views of the literary critic Charles Augustin Sainte-Beuve, who held that "one cannot be certain of having a complete grasp" of a writer without detailed biographical information. "Sainte-Beuve's method ignores what a very slight degree of self-acquaintance teaches us: that a book is the product of a different *self* from the self we manifest in our habits, in our social life, in our vices," Proust wrote. "If we would try to understand that particular self, it is by searching our own bosoms, and trying to reconstruct it there, that we may arrive at it. Nothing can exempt us from this pilgrimage of the heart." For Proust, the writer's authentic self is all that matters, and that authenticity can only be accessed through careful reading of the work itself. This "true voice of the heart" is sharply distinguished from mere "small-talk": "It is the secretion of one's innermost life, written in solitude and for oneself alone, that one gives to the public. What one bestows on private life . . . is the product of a quite superficial self, not of the innermost self which one can only recover by putting aside the world and the self that frequents the world."[16] Questionnaires, diverting as they are, record only small-talk.

Questions of aesthetic philosophy aside, the quarrel between Proust and Sainte-Beuve can be read as an early referendum on the value of the questionnaire in general. Do questionnaires capture something accurate and valuable about their subjects, which can be used to advance the public good? Or do they yield nothing more than gossip, "small-talk," "private publicity" fit for the drawing room but not the *demos*? Do we fill out questionnaires for the sake of society, or simply to see ourselves think on paper? In the coming century, all of the answers above would be given, in great quantities, and nowhere more so than in America.

2 TESTING, TESTING

In the United States, organizations glommed on to the questionnaire early. In the early decades of the twentieth century, most of the Americans who answered questionnaires were, in some way or another, forced to take them. Though the personal questionnaire began life as a tool of unaffiliated gentleman scientists like Francis Galton, it was quickly adopted by schools, universities, and other large organizations. Much early anthropometric research focused on the measurement of intelligence, a pursuit with obvious practical applications to mass education. In 1905, the French psychologists Alfred Binet and Théodore Simon developed a scale to measure the intelligence of children aged three to twelve. Lewis Terman, a psychology professor at Stanford, revised it in 1916 to create the Stanford-Binet Intelligence Scales, which in turn provided the model for the Scholastic Aptitude Test (SAT), the first national standardized intelligence test in the United States, introduced in 1926.

The adoption of self-report questionnaires by educational institutions was accompanied by a subtle but significant shift within the scientific community. Galton's questionnaires had been instruments for the collection of anthropometric data, which he and his followers used, in turn, to argue for the advancement of eugenic policies. Though the conclusions drawn from that data would affect the lives of millions, the consequences for the people who actually filled out Galton's forms were next to nil. Tests like the Binet-Simon, the Stanford-Binet, and the SAT, by contrast, were used for evaluative purposes, and thus had an immediate impact on the life chances of those who took them. Scoring low on an intelligence test, then as now, could get you barred from access to higher education or a white-collar job. It could also be aggregated with other scores and used to consign your entire race or ethnicity to subhuman status. For the first time, the questionnaire had become a tool not just for learning about people but also for sorting them.

Aside from the creation of the SAT, the most important moment in the early history of psychological testing came with America's mobilization for the First World War. In 1917, following the United States' entrance into the war, the American Psychological Association formed a Committee on the Psychological Examination of Recruits, chaired by APA President Robert Yerkes. Out of their inquiries came the famous Army Alpha and Beta Intelligence Tests, a series of multiple-choice examinations used to determine the "mental ability" of new draftees. The Alpha tests, routinely administered to groups as large as five hundred, combined various different kinds of arithmetical and verbal exercises in an attempt to measure overall intelligence. (The Beta tests were a nonverbal version for non-English speakers and the illiterate.) In addition to the Stanford-Binet scale and other tests of basic intelligence, recruits took tests of "practical judgment" that included multiple-choice questions like the following:

Why ought every man to be educated?   Because
☐   Roosevelt was educated
☐   it makes a man more useful
☐   it costs money
☐   some educated people are wise

Why is beef better food than cabbage?   Because
☐   it is harder to obtain
☐   it tastes better
☐   it is more nourishing
☐   it comes from animals

(The correct answers, in case you're struggling, are B and C.) A test of literacy administered to recruits at Fort Devens in Massachusetts began with short yes-or-no questions that were extremely simple in grammar and vocabulary ("Do dogs bark? Is coal white? Can you see?") and then advanced steadily in linguistic and semantic complexity ("Do clerks enjoy a vacation? . . . Do you cordially recommend forgery?"), before reaching a practically psychedelic pitch ("Are instantaneous effects invariably rapid? . . . Is an infinitesimal titanic bulk possible?").[1]

The immediate aims of the Alpha and Beta examinations were pragmatic: they allowed the Army to identify exceptional individuals who might be suited for officer training, and consign the lowest-scoring recruits to labor battalions and other menial posts. But the project also enabled psychologists to amass an unprecedented amount of anthropometric data on the American population. That data was, predictably, analyzed according to the prevailing eugenicist assumptions of the time. Yerkes's mammoth *Psychological Examining in the United States Army*, published in 1921, sorted soldiers according to race ("White" and "Negro," but also "black," "brown," and "yellow"-skinned subsets of the latter category) and place of origin. Whites scored higher than blacks across the board, and people born in the United States scored higher than those born in foreign countries. The Alpha tests were far from what we would now call "culture-blind": that is, what they measured was not "intelligence" (whatever that means) so much as familiarity with a specific cultural context. "Why ought every man to be educated?" is, of course, a question with more than one possible answer, but only "it makes a man more useful" was the *right* answer, in this case.

In scientific terms, as measurements of intelligence or ability, such tests are virtually useless. Nonetheless, the study's findings were almost immediately weaponized by the antiimmigrant nativist movement. In 1923, Yerkes contributed a foreword to the psychologist Carl C. Brigham's *A Study of American Intelligence*, which used the results of the Army Alpha and Beta examinations to argue for the superiority of the Nordic Race over the Alpine and Mediterranean and warn that "each succeeding five year period of immigration since 1902 has given us an increasingly inferior selection of individuals." "The author presents not theories or opinions but facts," Yerkes claimed. "It behooves us to consider their reliability and their meaning, for no one of us as a citizen can afford to ignore the menace of race deterioration or the evident relations of immigration to national progress and welfare."[2]

Writing for a popular audience in the *Atlantic Monthly* in the same year, Yerkes's nativism was even blunter: "Whoever desires high taxes, full almshouses, a constantly increasing number of schools for defectives, of correctional institutions, penitentiaries, hospitals, and special classes in our public schools, should by all means work for unrestricted and non-selective immigration," he wrote.[3] The next year, Congress passed the Johnson-Reed Immigration Act, which limited the number of immigrants allowed into the nation each year; eugenicists like Yerkes and Brigham were among its strongest supporters.

*

The end of the war did not spell the end of military psychological testing. In 1919, not long after the suspension of hostilities, the US military commissioned a questionnaire from the psychologist Robert S. Woodworth to address the problem of "shell shock." Fifteen thousand American veterans were reporting chronic nausea, heart palpitations, and other symptoms of what clinicians would now call Post-Traumatic Stress Disorder (PTSD). The severity of the epidemic led the Army to experiment with more rigorous screening of recruits for psychological instability, the governing assumption being that only the mentally weak would "crack up" under the strain of combat.

The test Woodworth developed—variously called the Woodworth Psychoneurotic Inventory, the Woodworth Psychopathic Questionnaire, and the Woodworth Personal Data Sheet—consisted of seventy-five yes-or-no questions. Some of these concerned physical characteristics: "Do you usually feel well and strong? . . . Do you have continual itchings in the face? . . . Are you bothered by fluttering of the heart?" Others addressed habits: "Does liquor make you quarrelsome? . . . Have you hurt yourself by masturbation (self-abuse?) . . . Did you ever have the habit of taking any form of 'dope'?" Many are, from a contemporary perspective, embarrassingly blatant attempts to identify pathological behavior: "Do you know of anybody who is trying to do you harm? . . . Do you ever have a queer feeling as if you were not your old self? . . . Do you feel like jumping off when you are on a high place? . . . Do you ever feel a strong desire to go and set fire to something?" And some simply seem intended to gage manly fortitude: "Can you sit still without fidgeting? . . . Can you stand pain quietly? . . . Do you like outdoor life?"[4]

Military examinations like the Army Alpha and the Woodworth demonstrated the utility of psychological testing on an institutional scale, and other types of institutions quickly took notice. Following the war, testing would become increasingly oriented toward the needs of industry. Organizations like The Scott Company and The Psychological Corporation, staffed by leading academic psychologists, set themselves up as paid consultants to corporate firms. Industrial, or "applied," psychology came into its own as a field, taking its place alongside Frederick Winslow Taylor's Scientific Management as a major influence on the culture of capitalist production.

The widely used Humm-Wadsworth Temperament Scale is a case in point. The "Humm" was the product of a collaboration between the psychologist Doncaster Humm and the personnel manager Guy Wadsworth, supposedly created in response to a disturbed employee's murder of his supervisor. The Humm's seven basic "Personality Syndromes"—"Hysteroid," "Manic," "Depressive," "Autistic," "Paranoid," "Epileptoid," and "Normal"—were borrowed from the work of the psychiatrist, and prominent eugenicist, Aaron Rosanoff, who had derived them from his work with patients at a New York state mental hospital. The test's yes-or-no structure resembles the Woodworth, but the questions were subtler, harder to "game," in part because there were now not just "psychopathic" and "normal" but seven potential factors of mental fitness in play. Certain motifs recur (obedience to authority, quarrelsomeness, religious enthusiasm) but, with 318 questions, there are inevitable red herrings and false alarms. How, for example, should the employee seeking to score "Normal" on the Humm-Wadsworth Temperament Scale answer question 29 ("When you hear a good story do you usually pass it on?"), or question 37 ("Should a man always boost his hometown against all others?")? Such workplace tests were more than un-culture-blind: they were elaborately designed traps that it was almost impossible not to fall into.

As severe as the Humm's pathologizing of the American workforce might appear to us today, from a management point of view of it made sense. While the politics of the early industrial psychologists were often relatively progressive— The Psychological Corporation's James McKeen Cattell, for example, corresponded with American Federation of Labor (AFL) founder Samuel Gompers about "how psychology could contribute to the goals of unionism"[5]—personality testing was a management science, and, like Taylorism, it was often put to antiunion purposes. The 1935 National Labor Relations Act made it illegal to ask prospective employees directly about union affiliations, but certain antisocial personality traits assumed to be linked to radicalism could be identified and used to screen out agitators and other troublemakers. Bosses, as the historian Michael Zickar notes, were "more likely to accept psychological explanations for the reasons why employees chose to join unions" than economic ones; it was cheaper to treat unionism as a psychological problem than it was to raise wages.[6]

Eventually, however, the techniques that management had cultivated in order to sort and control workers began to be applied to managers themselves. In the 1940s and 1950s, a series of "people-sorters" with unwieldy monikers—the Bernreuter Personality Inventory, the Worthington Personal History Blank, the Thurstone Personality Schedule, the Adams-Lepley Personal Audit, the Allport Ascendance-Submission Reaction Study, the Guilford-Zimmerman Temperament Survey—proliferated in the business world. By the time the journalist William H. Whyte published his 1956 polemic *The Organization Man*, such tests were familiar features of the corporate environment and, Whyte argued, evidence of the gray-flannel paralysis that was gripping it. "The use of psychological tests [in business] . . . is symptomatic," Whyte wrote:

> Originally, they were introduced by the managers as a tool for weeding out unqualified workers. As time went on, and personality tests were added to aptitude tests, the managers began using them on other managers, present and prospective, and today most personality testing is directed not at the worker, but at the organization man. If he is being hoist, it is by his own philosophy.

Like many other liberal midcentury intellectuals, Whyte worried that the spirit of American entrepreneurship was being smothered under a blanket of bureaucratic conformity. Personality tests, he feared, were encouraging "the organization man" to suppress his dynamic individuality and fit himself to an acceptably homogeneous profile. In the face of the Organization's invasive and stultifying testing regime, Whyte recommended a kind of civil disobedience: "When an individual is commanded by the organization to reveal his innermost feelings, he has a duty to himself to give answers that serve his self-interest rather than that of The Organization," he insisted. "In a word, he should cheat." *The Organization Man* even included a handy appendix, "How to Cheat on Personality Tests," which instructed aspiring organization men how "to answer as if you were like everybody else is supposed to be":

> To settle on the most beneficial answer to any question, repeat to yourself:
>
> a) I loved my father and my mother, but my father a little bit more.
> b) I like things pretty well the way they are.
> c) I never worry much about anything.
> d) I don't care for books or music much.
> e) I love my wife and children.
> f) I don't let them get in the way of company work.[7]

Whyte's book was a national bestseller, and it inaugurated a vicious cultural backlash against mandatory personality testing. Psychological tests at work began to seem like the epitome of totalitarian thought policing, and were thus susceptible to attack from both the left and the right as the 1960s wore on. "The obvious contest—man versus the testers—may be shaping up as the battle of the century," the libertarian critic Martin L. Gross fulminated in 1962's *The Brain Watchers*.[8] The American legal and political systems, too, began to turn against testing. The 1964 Civil Rights Act made companies reluctant to use tests that might be shown to have a systematic bias against minorities. In 1966, Senator Sam J. Ervin Jr. of North Carolina convened a hearing on *Privacy and the Rights of Federal Employees* that specifically targeted personality inventories as an unacceptable invasion of privacy.[9]

Perhaps the most important factor in the decline of psychological testing, however, was the steady drumbeat of scientific skepticism about its basic validity and value. Intelligence testing had been controversial from the beginning: it was opposed especially vociferously by anthropologists like Franz Boas, Margaret Mead, and Otto Klineberg, but also by journalists like Walter Lippmann and psychologists like the unfortunately named Edwin G. Boring. In 1930, C. C. Brigham, author of *A Study of American Intelligence*, disowned his previous research on intelligence completely, calling it "pretentious" and "without foundation."[10]

Eventually, similar criticisms began to be leveled at personality testing. In 1948, Bertram Forer published a paper in the *Journal of Abnormal and Social Psychology* titled "The Fallacy of Personal Validation: A Classroom Demonstration of Gullibility." In it, he described administering a questionnaire called the Diagnostic Interest Blank (DIB) to his class in introductory psychology at the Veterans Administration Mental Hygiene Clinic in Los Angeles. Forer told his students he would analyze the questionnaires and provide each of them with a unique personality sketch based on their test results. A week later, he passed out thirty-nine identical sketches, consisting of broad, quasi-universal statements like "You have a great need for other people to like and admire you" and "Some of your aspirations tend to be pretty unrealistic." He then asked his students to rate the test's effectiveness on a scale of 0 to 5. "Ratings of adequacy of the DIB included only one rating below 4," he noted. "All of the students accepted the DIB as a good or perfect instrument for personality measurement." Forer's point was that "personal validation"—the test taker's sense of a given personality test's overall accuracy—is an unreliable guide, a version of confirmation bias. "The positive results obtained by personal validation can easily lull a test analyst or a therapist into a false sense of security," he warned, "which bolsters his conviction in the essential rightness of his philosophy of personality or his diagnostic prowess."

The particular form of confirmation bias described in "The Fallacy of Personal Validation" would become known as the "Forer effect"—or sometimes the "Barnum effect," after the famed huckster P. T. Barnum. Though Forer didn't go quite so far as to accuse personality testers of charlatanism, he implied it by drawing a sly comparison between the personality tester and "the crystal-gazer."[11] (Slighting references to astrology are a staple of the scientific literature on personality testing.) A decade later, when the industrial psychologist Ross Stagner replicated Forer's experiment with a group of HR professionals for his article "The Gullibility of Personnel Managers," the polemical intent was more overt. "Psychological services are being offered for sale in all parts of the United States," Stagner wrote. "Some are bona fide services by competent, well-trained people. Others are marketing nothing but glittering generalities having no practical value." Stagner painted psychological consultants as con artists, deceiving naïve corporate managers by flattering their vanity: "Thus the shrewd salesman can easily dupe the personnel man, by appealing to his belief that his own judgment is better than statistics."[12]

The coup de grâce, from an academic perspective at least, was Walter Mischel's *Personality and Assessment*, published in 1968. In the most comprehensive and serious scientific critique of psychological testing to date, Mischel analyzed a wide range of personality instruments and concluded that the typical "personality coefficient"— that is, the correlation between test results and people's actual, observed behavior—was "a statistically significant but modest .30." "Although behavior patterns often may be stable, they usually are not highly generalized across situations," Mischel wrote in a later summary of his research. Furthermore, "discontinuities—real ones, not merely superficial or trivial surface changes—are part of the genuine phenomena of personality."[13] People change over time (sometimes), and behave inconsistently (often): these are genuine facts of human personality, not anomalies that a well-designed personality test or typological system can correct for. In Mischel's view, then, the fundamental premise of personality assessment—that individuals possess core psychological traits and attributes that remain consistent across different situations, contexts, and life stages—was simply wrong. All previous attempts to "test" for personality were based on a fundamental fallacy about human behavior, and should therefore be thrown out.

Testing had entered the mainstream of American life, thanks to the prestige of science. By 1970, it risked being ushered out the same way it had come in. In the wake of the work of Forer, Stagner, Mischel, and dozens of other debunkers, personality assessment became rather disreputable among academic psychologists. But psychological testing didn't disappear with the erosion of its scientific foundations. It simply became a vernacular idiom, thriving, for the most part, outside the formal institutional venues of the classroom and the laboratory. Tests like the MBTI and the Enneagram of Personality are taken, instead, at management seminars, New Age retreats, in church basements and the offices of quasi-religious organizations, and, almost immediately following the creation of the World Wide Web in 1989, online.

While many of the people who take and administer personality tests today still believe them to be, in some sense, "scientific," they are not likely to have a very high bar for the evidence to this effect. Moreover—and this is the really crucial difference—these tests are *voluntarily* taken. They are not trials that must be endured in order to land a job or attend a school but hobbies or passion projects pursued for one's own edification. Where most psychological tests in the first half of the twentieth century had been mandatory and officially imposed, today they are much more likely to be associated with smaller fringe organizations and devoted followings: cults, in every sense of the word.

3 YOUR OPINION OF YOU

The most popular personality test in the world today is the MBTI. Forty years ago, no one would have predicted its dominance. The MBTI has an unusual history. In 1923, an aspiring novelist named Katharine Cook Briggs read the psychoanalyst Carl Jung's treatise on *Psychological Types*. In this work, Jung distinguished between what he called "introverted" and "extroverted types": "The one sees everything in terms of his own situation, the other in terms of the objective event." He also evinced four "basic psychological functions . . . *thinking, feeling, sensation,* and *intuition*."[1] Logically, this produced eight different categories of people, since a thinking type could be either introverted or extroverted, and so on.

Briggs became an early popularizer of Jung's ideas in America. In 1926 she published an article entitled "Meet Yourself: How to Use the Personality Paint Box" in the *New Republic*. "To meet oneself through the good offices of Jung's theory of types is to be like the motorist who, after driving a car for years without knowledge of its mechanism, suddenly comes upon one of those cut-away engines and begins to understand the hows and whys of motor and transmission," she wrote. "A most valuable experience, especially to such as are dissatisfied with their mental powers and self-starters and gearshifts; and not too difficult if approached gradually and from the proper angle."

Elaborating slightly on Jung's original scheme, Briggs named "the *observant*, the *expectant*, the *personal*, and the *analytical*" as "the four primary character colors which each individual combines and blends according to his taste as he unconsciously paints in the detail of his own personality portrait, and thus reveals his type." While Jung propounded his theory of typology in the rather austere language of European psychoanalysis, Briggs presented it as a cheerful hobby for amateurs: "One need not be a psychologist in order to collect and identify types any more than one needs to be a botanist to collect plants. . . . The collector of types acquires a new conception of wholesome living, a new basis for the criticism and if necessary the reconstruction of his own life."[2]

Briggs's interest in personality type was humanistic: She thought Jung's system would make people happier, that it would be useful to artists and writers seeking to understand the human condition, and that it might have some application to progressive education. Her daughter Isabel Briggs Myers, by contrast, brought a more practical, technocratic emphasis to her mother's ideas. In the 1940s, Myers read an article in

Reader's Digest about the Humm-Wadsworth Temperament Scale entitled "Fitting the Worker to the Job." The MBTI, modeled on the Humm and other industrial "people-sorters" but grounded in Jungian type theory as opposed to the categories of eugenic psychiatry, was conceived as a career-placement tool that would help employers identify the strengths of job candidates and individuals find their proper line of work. It posited the existence of sixteen distinct personality types (doubling Jung's original eight), each made up of some combination of the following dimensions: Extroversion versus Introversion (E vs. I), Sensing versus Intuition (S vs. I), Thinking versus Feeling (T vs. F), and Judging versus Perceiving (J vs. P). Choosing one item from each of these menus produces a four-character type: I, for instance, am an Introverted Intuitive Feeling Perceiving (INFP), as are Princess Diana, Michel de Montaigne, J. K. Rowling, Anton Chekhov, and Stephen Colbert. Myers was convinced that the correct identification of these types would allow businesses to place their workers in the most suitable positions, thus increasing productivity and employee morale in one fell swoop.

The MBTI was tested first on Myers's friends and family—one of the first questions was "Do you prefer to (a) eat to live, or (b) live to eat"[3]—and, later, on students at Swarthmore College and at the George Washington School of Medicine. Beginning in 1962, it was carried by the Educational Testing Service, the publishers of the SAT, although it didn't really begin to catch on until it passed to the smaller but more aggressive and business-oriented Consulting Psychologists Press in 1975. (The CPP's slogan, circa 2015: "The people development people.") By 1980, when Isabel Myers died, the MBTI had sold a million copies; today it sells roughly $20 million per year, is available in more than twenty languages, and is widely used by management schools, government agencies, churches, colleges, and other organizations. Though the test itself is protected by copyright and can only be administered by those who have completed an expensive certification program, its basic categories have long been common coin, and the MBTI has a vocal fan base on the Internet. There are dozens of Myers-Briggs message boards and Facebook groups, and it has even inspired a kind of fan fiction: Tumblr sites like Funky MBTI in Fiction provide extensive MBTI profiles for characters from novels, films, and TV shows. (Emma Bovary, for example, is an INFP; Mad Max is an ISTP; Carrie from *Homeland* is an ENFJ.)

The massive popularity of the MBTI probably has a lot to do with the way it flatters those who take it. The test is designed to discover skills, not flaws: In the 1962 MBTI manual, for example, introverts are praised for their "depth and concentration," extroverts for their "ease with environment," the Feeling for their "sympathetic understanding and handling of people," and the Thinking for their "capacity for analysis and logic," etc. Of all of the personality tests developed in the twentieth century—and there have been hundreds—the MBTI is the closest to the language of pop psychology and self-help. "The Indicator's unfailingly positive tone blends seamlessly . . . with our society's emphasis on promoting self-esteem," the journalist Annie Murphy Paul has noted. She points to "Myers' deliberate focus on healthy, high-functioning individuals"— worlds away from the harsh, clinical judgments of the Humm. Myers's posthumous book about the development of the MBTI was entitled *Gifts Differing*, and, as Paul puts it, she had "an insistent belief that no one type was better than another, that everyone had a different set of 'gifts' to contribute to the world. . . . Each description was carefully crafted to avoid hurt feelings and injured vanity."[4] MBTI administrators are trained to emphasize the ecumenical, nonjudgmental character of the test, and its mass appeal is clearly linked to its feel-good, "all types are equal" message.

*

The positivity of the MBTI contrasts sharply with another of the twentieth century's longest-lived personality tests: the Oxford Capacity Analysis (OCA). The origins of the OCA are disputed, but all accounts agree that it was developed in the early 1950s at the behest of Scientology founder L. Ron Hubbard. Hubbard was fascinated by intelligence and personality tests, which were then very much in the scientific mainstream. In 1950, his Dianetic Research Foundation ran a battery of tests—including the Minnesota Multiphasic Personality Inventory, the California Test of Mental Maturity, and the Johnson Temperament Analysis (JTA's)—to try to establish the beneficial effects of dianetic auditing. (The results were inconclusive.)[5]

Soon, Hubbard was pushing for Scientology to develop its own personality test. This may, at first, have been a matter of necessity: In the mid-1950s, publishers of personality tests began to require their customers to be accredited by the American Psychological Association, thus cutting Hubbard off from access to more legitimate scientific instruments. But it also allowed the church to shape the test to its own institutional requirements. "The tests we need must be of a highly precise nature, depending on opinion [sic] of an operator not one bit," Hubbard wrote in a 1950 internal memo to his staff entitled "The Intensive Processing Procedure." "Our tests must be administerable [sic] to a small group simultaneously, must be graded swiftly, must contain a high degree of arithmetical estimation, and must present to a layman the facts and figures he expects of a science."[6]

To this end, Hubbard commissioned Julia Lewis, a Scientologist with a graduate degree in psychology, to craft a test based on the JTA's, a personality inventory developed in 1941 by a marriage clinic in Los Angeles. It appears that Lewis simply copied or paraphrased most of the JTA's questions, diagnostic categories, and scoring apparatus, introducing a few bizarre errors in the process (like the possibility of receiving negative percentile scores, which is mathematically impossible).

Lewis's test, which was copyrighted under her name in 1955, was called "the American Personality Analysis." In 1959, the test was revised, at Hubbard's instruction, by the British Scientologist Raymond Kemp and rebranded the "Oxford Capacity Analysis," in the apparent hope that the specious association with Oxford University would lend it an air of legitimacy outside the United States. The OCA has 200 questions. Some of them ("Do you browse through railway timetables, directories, or dictionaries just for pleasure? . . . Do you often sing or whistle just for the fun of it?") seem whimsical or irrelevant. Some are vaguely political ("Do you consider more money should be spent on social security? . . . Do you consider the modern 'prisons without bars' system doomed to failure?"). Others are obviously probing for signs of depression:

Are you rarely happy, unless you have a special reason?

Do you often "sit and think" about death, sickness, pain and sorrow?

Do you sometimes wonder if anyone really cares about you?

Would it take a definite effort on your part to consider the subject of suicide?

And several seem to aim at ferreting out those with cult potential:

Would you prefer to be in a position where you did not have the responsibilities of making decisions?

Could you agree, to strict discipline?

Would the idea of making a complete new start cause you much concern?[7]

Ultimately, though, the responses given to these particular questions don't matter very much, as it appears to be impossible to achieve a "good" score on the OCA. In 1971, the British government commissioned an investigation into Scientology. As part of the enquiry, several British psychologists took the OCA in London and Edinburgh, answering the questions randomly, and received "remarkably similar profiles" with uniformly low scores. They concluded that the test was rigged to produce a negative result. Moreover, they were appalled by the follow-up evaluations they were given after completing the tests, in which their supposed personality deficits were presented in the harshest possible light. "To report back a man's inadequacies to him in an automatic, impersonal fashion is unthinkable in responsible professional practice," the report reads. "To do so is potentially harmful. It is especially likely to be harmful to the nervous introspective people who would be attracted by the leaflet [for the test] in the first place." "The prime aim of the procedure seems to be to convince these people of their need for the corrective courses run by the Scientology organisations," the psychologists concluded.[8] Where the Myers-Briggs test flatters and protects those who take it, revealing to them their special psychological gifts, the Oxford Capacity

Analysis is designed to tear your personality down, in order to rebuild.

*

While I was researching this book, I read widely about the OCA. (As with all things Scientology, there's a tremendous amount of information about it on the Internet, not all of it trustworthy or unbiased.) But I wanted to see it for myself, and as luck would have it I live in Los Angeles, the Scientology capital of the world. On a sweltering day in August, I walked into the gigantic blue Church of Scientology building on Sunset Boulevard and asked to take a personality test. I was led into an open-plan office with Dianetics posters on the walls and a smattering of people conversing in English and Spanish. The OCA itself—200 questions that were roughly similar to what I had come across during my online research—took me a little under an hour to complete. After that I was given a half-hour IQ test and a timed "Aptitude Test" (seemingly a combination intelligence and personality test, which involved, among other tasks, writing my name in the left-hand margin of the page and circling it) that took me about five minutes.

Once my tests were scored, a pleasant woman in her mid-50s sat down with me and went over a line graph visualizing the results. The graph was divided into three layers: the top third was labeled "Desirable State," the middle "Normal," and the bottom "Unacceptable State." My chart looked like the EKG of a fading heart patient: for the most part, my data points were near the very bottom of the scale, with a couple of dramatic spikes indicting that I was "active" and "aggressive." What this meant, my evaluator told me, was that I was a very unhappy man. According to my OCA results, I was extremely nervous, irresponsible, and impulsive. I lived in my own head: always *thinking*. I didn't trust people or get along with them, and I could be critical, cold-blooded, and even heartless. But—here was the good news—I had a high aptitude score and an above-average intelligence, which meant I was capable of a lot more. Did I want to keep going down the same road I had been traveling, or did I want to change my life?

The OCA, I knew, was devised to provide troubling results of this sort. I also knew that the speech that my evaluator had just delivered—one that she gave every appearance of improvising on the spot based on the specifics of my chart— was basically a stock monologue. In a memo from 1959, Hubbard provided a script for OCA evaluators to follow, which begins: "Now let's look at your personality. This is what you've told us about yourself. Understand that this is not our opinion of you, but is a factual scientific analysis taken from your answers. It is your opinion of you."[9] The opinion that follows is always unremittingly negative, and it is always expressed in terms that, *mutatis mutandis*, sound very much like the ones I heard from my evaluator. The emphasis is on the test's neutrality and objectivity, and while the remedy is, conveniently, near at hand—just a couple of cubicles over, in my case, where another Scientologist tried in vain to get me to sign up for a four-day Dianetics course on "How to Improve Relationships with Others"—the diagnosis has come from the patient. "Your opinion of you," then, is that you are a problem only Scientology can solve.

The OCA is still used throughout the world as a recruiting tool for Scientology. Like almost everything about the church, it has been a source of controversy. In 2008, a Norwegian college student named Kaja Ballo committed suicide after taking the OCA, inciting a public furor over the test's demoralizing techniques in both Norway and France, where Ballo was living at the time.[10] French prosecutors were unable to establish a link between Ballo's suicide and Scientology, but she has since become a kind of martyr to European anti-Scientology activists.

I thought about Ballo as I sat in the Scientology building on Sunset, placidly listening to the verdict on my disaster of a personality. She, clearly, was one of those "nervous introspective people" the British psychologists worried might be especially susceptible to Scientology propaganda. What would she have felt, listening to a similar speech? Even if you are relatively mentally stable, you may find it distressing to hear someone you've just met rattle off a list of your flaws—some of which, inevitably, you will be inclined to agree with. (For the record: I *am* nervous! I *can* be impulsive!) It doesn't leave you feeling great about yourself; it's not meant to.

In my case, I knew that my evaluator was following, almost to the letter, a script that had been provided for her half a century ago and which, like the OCA itself, has remained essentially unchanged. But Ballo probably didn't know that. Suicides rarely stem from a single external cause, and it can be argued that, if the OCA didn't influence Ballo to take her own life, something else would have. But what if, instead of accepting a flyer from a Scientologist on the streets of Nice, she had logged onto her computer and taken a Myers-Briggs test instead? Would it have told her, maybe, that she was an INFP—an "Introverted Idealist"? That she shared a personality type with such notable cultural figures as William Blake, Virginia Woolf, John Lennon, and Isabel Briggs Myers herself? Would she have felt like she belonged? Was understood? She might not have felt any of this, or learned anything about herself that would have made her wiser or happier. But there are worse things than a waste of time.

4 THE ART OF ASKING

"What is the common man thinking?" George Gallup asks in the first sentence of the foreword to *The Pulse of Democracy*, his 1940 paean to the science of polling. "The life history of democracy can be traced as an unceasing search for an answer to this vital question."[1] With the birth of the scientific opinion poll, Gallup attests, the long search for that Holy Grail of representative democracy—an accurate gage of popular opinion—was finally reaching an end.

The questionnaire was a nineteenth-century European invention, honed in England and France and then exported to the United States where it was adopted by scientists and capitalists alike. But public opinion polling was a distinctively American enterprise. The first opinion surveys were undertaken around the turn of the century by churches affiliated with the Social Gospel movement; these tended to focus on problems facing local communities such as poverty and crime, and to have an explicitly reformist agenda. Around the same time, the sociologist W. E. B. Du Bois conducted a groundbreaking survey of Philadelphia funded by the University of Pennsylvania, also geared toward the identification and eradication of social problems.[2]

It was not until the 1930s, however, that American opinion polling really came into its own. Gallup was the preeminent pollster of his generation, and his surname remains the most famous one in opinion research to this day. ("Gallup poll," like "Xerox machine," is a brand name that's become familiar enough to assume the status of a universal.) Much of his lasting fame is due to the sheer force and persistence of Gallup's public relations efforts on behalf of his fledgling science. Some of the claims Gallup makes for opinion polling now seem outsized. In *The Pulse of Democracy*, he argues that careful, unbiased measurement of public opinion is one of the essential features that separate democracies like the United States from dictatorships like Nazi Germany and the Soviet Union. "The artificial creation of an apparent majority," such as those drummed up by the Nazis and the Soviets in order to pursue their ideological agendas, "provides a poor index of public opinion," Gallup writes.

> The vast majority of the American people feel in their bones that the case for dictatorship is riddled with weaknesses. . . . They are aware that the great flaw in the dictator's armor lies in his inability to know the real mind of his people, and that when he tries to get a true measure of public opinion, he is like a blind man groping in a dark room for a light that isn't there.[3]

Accurate opinion polling, by contrast, was the handmaiden of representative democracy.

But Gallup wasn't merely a propagandist for opinion polling; he was a methodological innovator as well. Though he studied social psychology at the University of Iowa with professors who could trace their intellectual lineage back to Galton and William James, his entrée to questionnaire research came when, while still a graduate student, he took a summer job at an advertising agency that was conducting a survey of newspaper readership in St. Louis. The self-report questionnaires that newspapers used to garner information on their readers were inadequate, Gallup realized, and for a simple reason: people lied on them. "I found that a high percentage of respondents claimed that they always read the editorials, the national and international news," he remembered later. "Few admitted to reading the gossip columns and other features of low prestige."[4] To correct for this flaw, he devised what would later become known as "the Gallup Method": essentially, sitting with the subject while they leafed through a newspaper in order to assess, based on their behavior, what they actually read.

These early consumer research experiments formed the basis for Gallup's 1928 PhD thesis, "An Objective Method for Determining Reader Interest in the Content of a Newspaper." They also brought him to the attention of the advertising agency Young & Rubicam, which hired him as their director of research in 1932. But Gallup's star as a statistician really began to rise when he successfully predicted Franklin Roosevelt's victory over Alf Landon in the 1936 presidential election. The *Literary Digest*, whose straw polls had correctly called every election since 1916, had Landon winning with 57 percent of the vote; Gallup had Roosevelt, with 55.7 percent. (In fact he won by even more: a decisive 60.8 percent.) It was a classic David and Goliath story: the *Digest*, which had been the leader in presidential straw polling for the past two decades, sent out some 20 million ballots in order to gage public opinion, while Gallup's poll relied on a sample of only about 50,000.[5]

The fact that a small, well-constructed sample could yield more accurate results than the brute-force count of a major media organization like the *Literary Digest* astonished the American public. In a chapter from *The Pulse of Democracy* entitled "Building the Miniature Electorate," Gallup patiently explains "the needlessness of piling up a large number of additional cases after a sample has achieved stability."[6] In order to demystify statistical sampling, he reaches for homely, everyday metaphors:

> The stenographer who hurriedly counts a single line of her typing to see how many words she has typed on the page is taking a rough "sample." The housewife, tasting a spoonful of tomato soup which she is preparing, "samples" the soup. The doctor who extracts a few cubic centimeters of blood from a vein in his patient's arm is taking a "sample" of the blood stream. In each case, a

part has been selected from the whole and subjected to analysis or measurement of one kind or another.[7]

Polls like the *Literary Digest*'s go wrong when they fail to account for the "character" of the cross section—that is, when they mistake the size of the polling audience for its representativeness of the whole. "Everyone knows that a representative sample of lemon pie, for instance," Gallup writes, "must include the meringue on top, the lemon in the middle, and the crust on the bottom. The *Literary Digest* sampling procedure in 1936 resembled the action of the small boy who eats the meringue on top and the lemon in the middle, but ignores most of the crust on the bottom"—that is, it overrepresented the wealthy and the middle class at the expense of the poor, who voted overwhelmingly for Roosevelt. *"No major poll in the history of this country ever went wrong because too few persons were reached,"* Gallup emphasizes (italics his): a counterintuitive claim at the time, but one that has been central to the science of survey and opinion research ever since.[8]

Gallup's electoral predictions made him a national celebrity. The organization he founded in 1935, the American Institute of Public Opinion, grew rapidly following its 1936 triumph, and he wrote a syndicated newspaper column called America Speaks! to disseminate its specific findings and proselytize for opinion polls in general. Businesses, particularly newspapers, invested heavily in polling technology, and academic social scientists found themselves in high demand for military and private-sector jobs.

But opinion polling had many critics as well, and their voices intensified after the embarrassing failure of the 1948 election, which Gallup and his fellow polling experts infamously called for Thomas Dewey. In 1949, the political scientist Lindsay Rogers, one of Gallup's fiercest critics, coined the epithet "pollster" on the analogy of "huckster."

Gallup—a pragmatist and a born wonk—responded to such criticisms by introducing more and more methodological refinements. Already in 1947, a year before the Dewey/Truman debacle, Gallup presented what he called his "quintamensional plan" of questionnaire design. Instead of one type of question—like the much maligned multiple-choice or "cafeteria" question pioneered by his fellow pollster Elmo Roper—Gallup proposed using five, which could be combined and analyzed using separate statistical methods to produce a richer, more accurate overall picture of public opinion.[9] When faced with criticism of polling, the remedies to be applied, in Gallup's opinion, were more, and better, polls.

*

Gallup's "Quintamensional Plan of Question Design" was only one of several midcentury works of social science that focused on the semantics of interrogation. The trend had been inaugurated in the mid-1930s by the Austrian sociologist and market researcher Paul Lazarsfeld; Lazarsfeld emigrated to the United States on a Rockefeller Foundation fellowship in 1933, and brought a rigorous, Vienna Circle-style logic to such mundane matters as movie theater attendance and coffee brand loyalty. In his seminal 1935 paper "The Art of Asking WHY in Marketing Research: Three Principles Underlying the Formulation of Questionnaires," Lazarsfeld made an early attempt to root out ambiguity and imprecision in question design. "Our program is to find out: 'Why did you buy this book?'" Lazarsfeld wrote in order to illustrate what he called "the principle of specification":

> A respondent will give, out of the same concrete experience, quite different answers, according to the particular word stressed: BUY, THIS, and BOOK. If he understood: "Why did you BUY this book?", he might answer, "Because the waiting list in the library was so long that I shouldn't have got it for two months." If he understood: "Why did you buy THIS book?" he might tell what interested him especially in the author. If he understood: "Why did you buy this BOOK?" he might report that he at first thought of buying a concert ticket with the money but later realized that a book is a much more durable possession than a concert, and such reasoning caused him to decide upon the book.

A good questionnaire, Lazarsfeld insisted, would specify *precisely* what it wanted to know, and make sure the respondents properly understood it. "We cannot leave it up to the respondents to tell us whatever they are inclined," he wrote. "The real task . . . which confronts the market student every time he starts out . . . is to be constantly aware of what he really means or seeks to discover by his questionnaire."[10]

Lazarsfeld brought the epistemological sophistication of Austrian philosophy to marketing research. In his eyes, "the consumer purchase became a special case of a problem which had great sanctity in the European humanistic tradition: *Handlung*, action."[11] Throughout the 1930s and 1940s, he directed a series of ambitious but underfunded research centers, usually affiliated with academic institutions but reliant on commissions from business to survive; studies produced during this time include "Should Bloomingdale's Maintain Its Restaurant," "Exploratory Study of the Psychology of Refrigerator Purchasers," and "The Buying of Vitamin Preparations."[12] This was a sharp sideways turn for a scholar who, as a young man, had been active in the Socialist Student Movement and whose early work had, in his own estimation, "a visible Marxist tinge." Lazarsfeld's first book, *Jugend und Beruf (Youth and Profession)*, published in 1931, was a sociological study of how young people of different classes decided on what career to pursue. In fact, Lazarsfeld had originally wanted to study not the occupational choices but the voting behavior of young people: "The Austro-Marxist position put all hope on the winning of elections rather than on the Communist belief in violence, and therefore there was great interest in how people voted," he remembered decades later. But since a study of leftist politics would have been controversial at the "dogmatically conservative" University of Vienna, "as a conscious substitute, I turned to the question of how young people develop their occupational plans."

One substitution of object—Lazarsfeld's substitution of occupational choice for voting—soon led to another, when one of his Viennese graduate students was asked by an American company to conduct marketing research on Austrians' preferred brands of soap. "I immediately linked [marketing research] up with my problem of occupational choice," Lazarsfeld recalled. "Obviously, my difficulty was that such choices extended over a long period of time, with many ramifications and feedbacks. If I wanted to combine statistical analysis with descriptions of entire choice processes, I had better, for the time being, concentrate on more manageable material. Such is the origin of my Vienna market research studies," he concludes grandly, "the result of the methodological equivalence of socialist voting and the buying of soap."

In 1937, Lazarsfeld became director of the Princeton Radio Research Project, funded by a grant from the Rockefeller Foundation, with a mandate to study the effects of mass communication and propaganda. Again, the research had a commercial orientation, but Lazarsfeld managed to smuggle some subversive elements into the mix as well. The most famous example is his recruitment of the radical German philosopher Theodor Adorno, whom he invited to travel to the United States in 1938 to head up a study of radio music. Lazarsfeld was "intrigued by his writings on the 'contradictory' role of music in our society" and "considered it a challenge to see whether I could induce Adorno to try to link his ideas with empirical research."[13]

Not surprisingly, this proved difficult. Adorno, trained in the speculative tradition of German philosophy, was suspicious if not entirely dismissive of empirical sociological work. "I considered it to be my fitting and objectively proffered assignment to *interpret* phenomena—not to ascertain, sift, and classify facts and make them available as information," he writes in a 1960 memoir of this period. Adorno was disturbed by the Radio Project researchers' lack of interest in aesthetics and by their tendency to think of musical works as mere "stimulus." He was also, at least initially, uncomfortable with questionnaires. "I immersed myself in observations of American musical life, especially the radio system, and set down theories and hypotheses about it; but I could not construct questionnaires and interview-schemes that would get to the heart of the matter," he recalled. Though he gamely tried to conform to the research style of his American hosts, he was, privately, skeptical about the entire enterprise: "I . . . hardly knew whether the questions that I regarded as essential could be done justice to by questionnaires. To tell the truth, I still don't know," he wrote in 1960.

The whole project of opinion research is predicated on the assumption that people can tell you what they really think. They may be reluctant or confused, but once you get past their defenses and clarify your intent, they will "open up" and give you the straight dope. Adorno, steeped as he was in Marxist theories of ideology and Freudian theories of the unconscious, didn't believe in such easy transparency. According to him, most people couldn't tell you what they really thought even if they *wanted* to. "The apparently primary, spontaneous reactions [of survey respondents] were insufficient as a basis for sociological knowledge because they were themselves conditioned," he wrote. In Adorno's view, society was "a totality that not only operates upon people from without but [which] has long been internalized": it got under people's skin and into their brains. To assume that simply asking questions, no matter how artfully phrased, would furnish accurate sociological data was hopelessly naïve.

To say the least, Adorno did not get along with his co-workers at the Radio Project. Most of them found him alien and pretentious, and he in turn thought them vulgar and unimaginative. Everywhere around him, he saw instances of preformatted, standardized, stereotyped thought, what he called "ticket thinking" (*Ticketdenken*):

Among the frequently changing colleagues who came into contact with me in the Princeton Project was a young lady. After a few days she came to confide in me and asked in a completely charming way, "Dr. Adorno, would you mind a personal question?" I said, "It depends on the question, but just go ahead." And she continued, "Please tell me: are you an extrovert or an introvert?" It was as if she was already thinking, as a living being, according to the pattern of the so-called "cafeteria" questions on questionnaires, by which she had been conditioned.

*

Adorno left the Radio Research Project in 1941, having produced a few significant theoretical texts but little in the way of viable empirical research. This was not the end of his adventures with the questionnaire format, however. In 1945, he was invited to participate in a research project on anti-Semitism being conducted by a group of psychologists at the University of California at Berkeley. This line of investigation eventually spawned *The Authoritarian Personality*, one of the landmark works of midcentury social science. This gargantuan study, which runs to nearly 1,000 pages, was conceived in reaction to the rise of fascism in Europe throughout the 1930s and 1940s. The authors wanted to know, in particular, whether something like Nazi ideology would ever be able to take root in the United States as it had in Germany, and what kind of American citizens might be most susceptible to it. To this end they devised "the F-scale," which purported to measure the potential for fascist sympathies in individual personalities.

Intriguingly, the inspiration for the F-scale seems to have come, at least in part, from the mass media that Adorno famously despised. "Certain tests in American magazines," he later recalled, "suggested to us the idea that without expressly asking about anti-Semitic and other fascistic opinions, one could indirectly determine such tendencies by establishing the existence of certain rigid views, of which one can be fairly certain that in general they accompany these particular opinions and constitute with them a characterological unity." This assumption—that one could identify fascists more effectively by asking oblique, indirect questions than by confronting their ideological prejudices head on—freed Adorno and his colleagues to let their imaginations run wild: they "spent hours thinking up entire dimensions, variables, and syndromes, including particular questionnaire items, of which we were all the prouder the less they betrayed their relationship to the main theme."[14]

The questionnaires used for *The Authoritarian Personality* were specifically designed to get around the problem of "spontaneous response" that had troubled Adorno when he worked for the Princeton Radio Research Project. "Opinions, attitudes, and values, as we conceive of them, are expressed more or less openly in words," the book's introduction reads.

> Psychologically they are "on the surface." . . . It is to be recognized, however, that the individual may have "secret" thoughts which he will under no circumstances reveal to anyone else if he can help it; he may have thoughts which he cannot admit to himself, and he may have thoughts which he does not express because they are so vague and ill-formed that he cannot put them into words.

This theory of "secret" versus "surface" thoughts accounts for the distinctively psychoanalytic approach that Adorno and his collaborators took to designing questionnaires and interview questions: "To gain access to these deeper trends is particularly important," they wrote, "for precisely here may lie the individual's potential for democratic or antidemocratic thought and action in crucial situations." Where Gallup believed that filtering out the uninformed and adding qualitative context could produce better questionnaire results, and Lazarsfeld felt that it was only a matter of perfecting the phrasing, Adorno and his coauthors believed that it was up to social scientists to interpret the *real* meaning behind their respondents' answers, much as a Freudian analyst or literary critic would.

F-scale questionnaires were distributed to college students, psychiatric clinic patients, public school teachers, merchant marine officers, San Quentin inmates, and others, mostly in the San Francisco Bay Area. No one, apart from a few leaders of liberal organizations, was told the real purpose of the study; it was presented to the respondents as "a survey of general public opinion, 'like a Gallup poll.'" Subjects were later selected for additional one-on-one interviews based on their questionnaires. Alongside some factual and open-answer questions, the original form comprised a series of "antidemocratic statements with which the subjects were invited to agree or disagree" on an "opinion-scale" of one to six. The first round of questionnaires used fairly blatant statements of prejudice to measure anti-Semitism ("Jewish power and control in money matters is far out of proportion to the number of Jews in the total population"), ethnocentrism ("The Negroes would solve many of their social problems by not being so irresponsible, lazy, and ignorant"), and politico-economic conservatism ("It is a fundamental American tradition that the individual must remain free of government interference, free to make money and spend it as he likes"). Based on these results and subsequent follow-up interviews, Adorno and his collaborators assembled a second collection of statements to measure the potential for fascism. This was the F-scale, an extraordinary document that reads more like a Brecht monologue than a typical scientific questionnaire. Entries included:

Although many people may scoff, it may yet be shown that astrology can explain a lot of things.

Too many people today are living in an unnatural, soft way; we should return to the fundamentals, to a more red-blooded, active way of life.

After we finish off the Germans and Japs, we ought to concentrate on other enemies of the human race such as rats, snakes, and germs.

Familiarity breeds contempt.

One should avoid doing things in public which appear wrong to others, even though one knows that these things are really all right.

He is, indeed, contemptible who does not feel an undying love, gratitude, and respect for his parents.

Novels or stories that tell about what people think and feel are more interesting than those which contain mainly action, romance, and adventure.

Homosexuality is a particularly rotten form of delinquency and ought to be severely punished.

There is too much emphasis in college on intellectual and theoretical topics, not enough emphasis on practical matters and on the homely virtue of living.

No matter how they act on the surface, men are interested in women for only one reason.

The sexual orgies of the old Greeks and Romans are nursery school stuff compared to some of the goings-on in this country today, even in circles where people might least expect it.

No insult to our honor should ever go unpunished.

There are some things too intimate or personal to talk about even with one's closest friends.

What a man does is not so important so long as he does it well.

When you come right down to it, it's human nature never to do anything without an eye to one's own profit.

No sane, normal, decent person could ever think of hurting a close friend or relative.[15]

How effective such cryptic statements might be in pinpointing latent fascist tendencies is arguable, though hundreds of pages of *The Authoritarian Personality* are devoted to exactly this. Among the statistical variables extracted from the respondents' reactions to these statements are "Conventionalism," "Authoritarian submission," "Superstition and stereotypy," and "Destructiveness and cynicism." While few, if any, of Adorno's findings would stand up today in the fields of sociology, psychology, or political science, *The Authoritarian Personality* was taken very seriously in its time. The F-scale, in particular, was adopted by quite a few experimental psychologists and sociologists, and remained in the repertoire of the social sciences well into the 1960s.

Today, the study is often criticized, and rightly, for its overt political bias. Adorno and his collaborators began by assuming that the people attracted to fascist ideas were pathological, and everything flowed from that initial negative value judgment. This in itself is ironic enough, given Adorno's hatred of predetermined stereotypes and "ticket thinking." But there is another irony here, one that Adorno himself, had he been able to see it, might have called "dialectical." If something like the F-scale were to fall into the wrong hands, couldn't it become a vehicle of tyranny? Couldn't Adorno's antiauthoritarian research on authoritarianism potentially lend itself to exactly the kind of state manipulation of the individual that authoritarian fascism is built upon? Being able to categorize citizens according to personality type, and to predict which types might be most receptive to certain policy initiatives, would obviously be a powerful tool for a dictator, even if the categories were only roughly accurate. For all of the easy points Gallup scores off the Nazis and the Soviets, he's right that "the artificial creation of an apparent majority" is a key weapon in the totalitarian arsenal, and it isn't clear why something like the F-scale, were it to be adopted by a fascist state, couldn't be used to this end.

What Adorno's bold, flawed experiment in survey research finally shows is how hard it is to predict the politics of the questionnaire in advance. Asking questions can have any number of unintended consequences, even when you think you know what the answers will be ahead of time. A radical leftist could, with the best of intentions, help craft a new instrument of fascist control, while a social conservative might well create a machine for feminist liberation, as we will see in the following chapter. It's as if the objects, once fashioned, have minds of their own, like Hans Christian Andersen's red shoes or the One Ring from *Lord of the Rings*. If the notion of "spontaneous response" is one kind of ideological illusion, the faith that a master theorist can decode the truth behind subjects' statements is another. It's much more likely that history will give them a meaning that neither foresaw.

5 PANDORA'S CHECKLIST

The rise of the personal questionnaire broadly parallels the rise of women's literacy, which soared across class divisions in the late nineteenth and early twentieth centuries. In the Victorian era, as we've already seen, women were singled out for questioning. Galton went after mothers with his *Record of Family Faculties*; the makers of confession albums sold them to ladies of leisure, who did the work of coaxing men to join in the game. Survey research began as a feminine endeavor, too. Many of the Social Gospel's volunteer canvassers were female parishioners, and the American Institute of Public Opinion often employed women interviewers, in part because they could be paid less—Gallup was infamously stingy with compensation—but also because it was believed that women were more skillful at coaxing responses out of hesitant subjects. "Almost all our interviewers are women," Gallup told a reporter for the *St. Petersburg Times* in 1976. "They do a better job. They follow directions better and people are really less reluctant to talk with a woman, and women are much more conscientious."[1]

If women were reckoned better at posing sensitive questions than men, they were also, it was thought, more willing to answer them. Victorian stereotypes about female narcissism and volubility carried over into the twentieth century, where they would be imported into a variety of contexts, both scientific and popular. Housewives, in particular, were the objects of almost obsessive attention by midcentury marketers, who identified them as the true seat of purchasing power in the average American household. The omnipresence of such consumer surveys was satirized by the comedian Stan Freberg in a 1960 television commercial for Cheerios:

HOUSEWIFE: Well, I used to have these terrible headaches, right here at the temple, and then I heard about Cheerios, and . . .

INTERVIEWER: No, no—Cheerios are not a headache remedy.

HOUSEWIFE: I'm sorry, I thought you were from a different company! I've been interviewed so much lately I just got confused.

INTERVIEWER: No, Cheerios are a breakfast cereal.

HOUSEWIFE [nodding]: My kids eat them *all the time*.[2]

Why so many questions for women in this period? One reason, perhaps, is that, in the wake of suffrage in 1920 and the ongoing struggles for emancipation fought by both first- and second-wave feminists, the proper conduct of women's lives was up in the air in a way it had not been for generations. "What does a woman want?" Freud famously asked in a letter of 1925. In those years, confusion about what exactly women wanted, or were supposed to want, was pervasive. It extended both to male experts, whose extant protocols for treating or selling to women were rapidly passing their sell-by dates, and to women themselves, who often reacted to the new freedoms offered by feminism with a mixture of excitement and terror: by asking and answering specific questions, some of the terror could be contained. The results of a diagnostic test, for instance, could reassert a kind of patriarchal authority by telling you what type you were, and what you ought to do. But the excitement could also be channeled into new ways of thinking about gender, marriage, and society. Questionnaires, then, could be mechanisms of psychological control, but also portals to self-reflection, instruments of what the women's movement of the 1970s would call "consciousness-raising."

Initially, though, the emphasis fell squarely on the dangers presented to society by unchecked female sexuality. Once again, eugenicists played a decisive role, and pressed the questionnaire into the service of their political agenda. Many of the gender debates in the first half of the twentieth century centered (as they do today) on marriage and reproduction, and in particular the fear that feminism might distract or dissuade young women from becoming wives and mothers. The eugenic version of this argument went like this: If women refused to get married and have children—particularly the white, upper- and upper-middle-class women whose offspring were assumed to be the most intelligent and socially useful—then the American genetic stock would inevitably be overwhelmed by the children of "inferior" races and steadily deteriorate. Such a turn of events would be tantamount to "race suicide," a phrase bandied about liberally in early-twentieth-century eugenicist circles.

One of the most prominent proponents of the "race suicide" hypothesis was a man named Paul Popenoe, now best remembered as the father of American marriage counseling. Popenoe began his career studying agriculture—his first published work was on date farming—but he soon became more interested in the cultivation of human beings. In 1918, he coauthored a college textbook on *Applied Eugenics* with the University of Pittsburgh professor Roswell Hill Johnson. In the 1920s, he undertook an extensive study of California's compulsory sterilization laws, which resulted in a book with the self-explanatory title *Sterilization for Human Betterment*. (California's statutes would subsequently provide a model for the German Law for the Prevention of Hereditarily Diseased Offspring, passed by the Third Reich in 1933. Popenoe publicly praised the German laws, and also spoke highly of Hitler's *Mein Kampf*.)[3]

Though he never really abandoned it, Popenoe downplayed his commitment to eugenics as public sentiment turned against scientific racism in the post-World War II period. Indeed, even before the war, he had begun to focus increasingly on "positive," as opposed to "negative," eugenics:

that is, on encouraging "superior" individuals to marry and reproduce, rather than instituting medical procedures for the elimination or sterilization of the mentally and physically "inferior." In 1926, Popenoe published *The Conservation of the Family*, a book that argued strenuously for the consolidation of the institution of marriage, which he saw as under threat from feminism, industrialization, and a host of other modern evils. "I began to realize that if we were going to promote a sound population," he later recalled, "we would not only have to get the right kind of people married, but we would have to keep them married."[4] Successful eugenics would have to involve not just snipping private parts but winning hearts and minds as well.

With this civilizing mission in mind, Popenoe founded the American Institute of Family Relations (AIFR), the nation's first marriage clinic, in Pasadena, California, in 1930. Each year, thousands of people—mostly engaged and married couples, but also children, expectant parents, and single people—visited the Institute, where they submitted to a battery of tests and questionnaires. The most important instrument of measurement at the AIFR was the JTA's, designed specifically for the Institute by Roswell Hill Johnson in 1941. The JTA's had 182 questions, and it sorted respondents according to a series of nine opposed pairs: Nervous-Composed, Depressive-Gay Hearted, Active-Quiet, Cordial-Cold, Sympathetic-"Hard Boiled," Subjective-Objective, Aggressive-Submissive, Critical-Appreciative, and Self-Mastery-Impulsive. (This was the test that would later provide the model for Scientology's OCA: Julia Lewis merely swapped out different oppositional categories for Johnson's. A modified form of the JTA's—known as the Taylor-JTA's—is still in circulation today.)

The JTA's measured psychological traits like introversion and extroversion, but its primary concern was with the degree of congruence between socialized gender characteristics and anatomical sex. "A proximate correspondence between sex and gender equaled normal," the historian Alexandra Stern writes, "while distance and deviation [from the norm] indicated conditions stretching from minor and fixable gender distortion to nearly fatal gender pathology." The personality traits the test associated with masculinity and femininity were, to say the least, stereotypical: men, on average, were "active, venturesome, aggressive, consistent, nomadic, businesslike, secular, rational, high-minded, and courageous"; women were "modest, submissive, romantic, sincere, religious, vindictive, 'catty,' drawn to trivia, and affectionately demonstrative." Female clients were frequently diagnosed with "masculine protest" (i.e., aggressiveness, often indicated by a belief in equality between the sexes) or frigidity (a trait determined by their statistical position on "the Cordial-Cold axis"). Stern notes that "the JTA's statistical assumptions and assessment protocols allowed men much greater deviation [from the norm] than women": even the *math* behind the JTA's was sexist.[5]

Though the AIFR was a clinical institution first and foremost, it also conducted research. Throughout the 1930s and 1940s the Institute kept journalists supplied with "findings" like the fact that mothers-in-law are meddlers, or that women who work outside the home are "spoiled" for romantic relationships. Popenoe, who had briefly edited a newspaper around the turn of the century, made for a natural pundit, and he was particularly adept at pandering to the conventional sexism of the period while soft-pedaling his more extreme eugenic beliefs. "Femaleness is protracted childhood. The eternal feminine is the eternal juvenile," he said in a 1934 lecture, a remark that was widely and approvingly quoted in newspapers of the time.[6]

Despite the obvious misogyny of many of Popenoe's statements, it appears that the bulk of his audience was made up of women. Two long-running advice columns appeared widely under his name: "Modern Marriage," which was syndicated in newspapers across the country from 1947 to 1972, and "Can This Marriage Be Saved?," which premiered in the *Ladies' Home Journal* in 1953 and is still running today. Soon other marriage counselors were publishing similar columns, which often included questionnaires and quizzes intended to measure marital satisfaction. Here, for instance, are some representative yes-or-no questions from "Ask Yourself: 'Is My Marriage Happy?'," a quiz printed in Clifford R. Adams's "Making Marriage Work" column in the *Ladies' Home Journal* in January 1948:

Do either of you have habits to which the other objects?

Is anything in your marriage especially unsatisfactory to you?

Do you ever wish you had never married?

Do you *rarely* have misunderstandings about money matters?

Are you two about equally loving and affectionate?

Do you live without interference from in-laws?

Are you two well-adjusted sexually?

Do you have much the same ideas about children?

Can you freely talk things over without reservations?

Are you free from debt and financial stress?

Do you believe your marriage to be successful?[7]

This checklist—one of hundreds of similar questionnaires that appeared in the pages of family newspapers and women's magazines during the long heyday of marriage counseling—gives a good sense of how this ambiguous discourse worked. On the one hand, marital satisfaction is presented as the be-all and end-all of female existence. On the other, the questions hardly let the husbands off the hook: they encourage women to demand at least a limited form of equality ("Are you two about equally loving and affectionate?") and a baseline of respect and reciprocity ("Can you freely talk things over without reservations?")

In documents like this, we see how the fundamentally conservative enterprise of marriage counseling made some accidental contributions to women's liberation nonetheless. As retrograde as Popenoe and other self-styled marriage experts were in many of their assumptions about femininity, they also helped cultivate a society in which women felt increasingly comfortable speaking up about their marital and sexual desires and dissatisfactions. The historian Molly Ladd-Taylor notes that the eugenic goal of "getting 'normal' women to want more children . . . meant confronting wives' dissatisfaction with marriage," and much of the counseling offered by the AIFR encouraged husbands to be more attentive to their wives' needs and desires.[8]

Then there's the fact that, as with any text, the author cannot control the uses readers make of it. In 1960, a 26-year-old Joan Didion wrote a tongue-in-cheek appreciation of "Making Marriage Work" for *National Review*, pointing out the extent to which such columns were consumed by women outside their ostensible audience: "The fact that I am unmarried has never deterred me from taking—and, with relentless regularity, failing—the *Journal*'s monthly 'Making Marriage Work' test."[9] In Didion's estimation, the basic message of these columns was that "men can be handled. This handling, this marital know-how, is the basis of all women's magazine marriage counseling." Not quite a call for sexual revolution, but still, in its canny assignment of agency to the female takers of such tests, a long way from "the eternal feminine is the eternal juvenile."

*

Marriage counseling opened the Pandora's box of female desire, and the questionnaire—or, more specifically, the quiz—quickly became the most popular device for naming, enumerating, and organizing all that had been set free. The first recognizable versions of the women's magazine quiz, as we know it today, began to appear in the mid-1960s in the pages of *Cosmopolitan*. Helen Gurley Brown became the magazine's first female editor in July 1965, and immediately began tailoring it toward the kind of aspirational modern woman she had described in her 1962 bestseller *Sex and the Single Girl*, an ideal construct she would soon dub "the *Cosmo* girl." Quizzes played an important role in defining this hypothetical individual. The first feature in Brown's magazine that really resembles the fully evolved "*Cosmo* quiz" was "How well do you know yourself?," published in the summer of 1966.[10] While still attributed to a male expert—in this case, Dr. Ernest Dichter, a Viennese psychologist best known for applying Freudian theory to consumer research—the focus here was not on marital adjustment but on introspection and self-knowledge.

Quizzes quickly became a regular feature of *Cosmopolitan*. The typical "*Cosmo* quiz" combined the clinical scrutiny of marriage counselors like Popenoe and Adams with the language of consciousness, positivity, and empowerment that was so important to second-wave feminism. *Cosmopolitan's Hangup Handbook*, an anthology published in 1971, is structured around six "barometer" quizzes covering the various "*patterns* that make your days fair or cloudy." There is a Believe-in-You Barometer (sample question: "Did you pass up a good thing for a *safe* thing?"), an Affair Barometer ("Are you *still* waiting for him to shed his wife?"), a Fun-in-Bed Barometer ("Are you timid about letting him know your sexual needs?"), an Emotional Barometer ("Have you said or thought 'It's all *my* fault' more than once this week?"), a Coping Barometer ("Have you spent more than a total of two hours seriously plotting revenge?"), and a Liberation Barometer ("Did you play dumb or refuse to argue for fear he'd think that you were being 'unfeminine'?") On the back of the book jacket was printed "the Weekly-Monthly-Semiannual-Yearly-Good-for-a-Lifetime Coordinated Hangup Barometer," which the readers were encouraged to cut out and "pin . . . or hang . . . up where you generally fall into your introspective trances." The book's final instructions: "Don't self-destruct . . . self-*evaluate*. Good luck!"[11]

Cosmopolitan's Hangup Handbook gives a good sense of how Brown's magazine threaded the needle when it came to feminism. Certainly, it was necessary to respond somehow to the challenges represented by the movement. Feminists had been attacking women's magazines since at least the publication of Betty Friedan's *The Feminine Mystique* in 1964, and radical opposition to the mass media's representation of women mounted over the course of the sixties. In March 1970, a group of over a hundred feminist activists, led by Signe Hammer and Susan Brownmiller, occupied the offices of the *Ladies' Home Journal* and demanded, among other things, the immediate cancellation of Popenoe's "Can This

Marriage Be Saved?" column. (When the group was allowed, as a concession, to edit a special section in the August 1970 issue, they ran a parody called "Should This Marriage Be Saved?"; the answer was a resounding no.)[12] Later that same year, Brown's own office was occupied by a feminist group led by the literary scholar Kate Millett; though Brown insisted that *Cosmopolitan* was "already a feminist book," she agreed to attend a consciousness-raising session along with other *Cosmo* staffers. "Twelve of us—I almost said girls, but they say I must stop that and refer to us as women—sat about and related our hangups," Brown remembered. "Frankly, I was only into my eighth hangup when I had to relinquish the floor to the next hangup-ee."[13]

Though Brown's tone here is decidedly facetious, *Cosmo* did take some of second-wave feminism's challenges to heart. In November 1970, shortly after the occupation, they published a long excerpt from Millett's *Sexual Politics* critiquing the Freudian concept of penis envy. Moreover, *Cosmopolitan's Hangup Handbook* incorporated the rhetoric of feminist protest into its very title. But while Brown and the other editors of *Cosmopolitan* were less befuddled by the movement than John Mack Carter, the clueless male editor of the *Ladies' Home Journal*, they tended to treat it not as a revolutionary movement but as a new species of self-help. For the *Cosmo* girl, feminism was less a demand to transform social structures or win legal and political rights for women than a powerful new lens through which she could "self-evaluate." "Think a minute about the hangups you've hoped to iron out (or at least *uncrease* a little!) by reading this book," the editors exhort their readers in the introduction to the "Liberation" section of *Cosmopolitan's Hangup Handbook*. "It's possible that some of the 'neurotic' symptoms which beset you are simply *normal* reactions to second-sex status. . . . Such 'sexism' *can* explain *many* of life's harassments, and we have Women's Liberation to thank for this plausible supplement to our problem-analyzing artillery."

There is something genuinely liberating in this suggestion that what seem like neuroses or "hangups" may actually be perfectly normal human reactions to an unjust society. But there's also something deflating in *Cosmopolitan's* insistence that feminism is nothing but a "plausible supplement to our problem-analyzing artillery": a new thing to worry about, or a new way to worry, even if that worry is almost immediately relieved. Not to mention the fact that analysis of problems was meant to lead, not to social or institutional reform, but to the old positive eugenic goal of better, stronger marriages: "In this mood, then, read on . . . not as a conspirator against an arbitrary enemy, but as a sister to your sex," the editors enjoin the lib-curious *Cosmo* girls. "These revolutionary ideas may mean happier times for you *and* your man!"[14]

What the *Cosmo* quiz did was fuse the apparent rigor of the marriage test with the feel-good feminism of the consciousness-raising session. As with the confession album (a form that the *Cosmo* quiz resembles in many respects), the goal was the minute inspection of individuality. The relentless examination of the self was what united the scientific enterprise of marriage counseling and the frivolous pastime of women's magazine quizzes. Both Popenoe and Brown wanted women to think deeply about who they were and what they wanted, and while the former aimed to direct and suppress many of those unruly desires, the latter at least paid lip service to ideals of freedom and self-determination.

But if *Cosmo* quizzes were feminist tools of a sort, they were imperfect ones, designed primarily for commercial rather than political purposes. (As Audre Lorde put it, "The master's tools will never dismantle the master's house"; perhaps the same goes for the master's tests?) "There is no doubt," the critic Susan J. Douglas writes, "that as these magazines demanded increased self-scrutiny—so important to selling cosmetics, clothes, and Relaxacizors—they also exaggerated our psychic schizophrenia, our sense of being a mosaic of traits that didn't quite fit together." She considers the quizzes "especially insidious. They always addressed us directly and intimately as 'you,' as if they were personally designed for each and every one of us. They asked us a lot of personal questions and invited us to confess—in private, of course, and to an understanding listener who would never tell anyone. And they promised enhanced self-knowledge if you'd only pick up a pencil and check off a few answers."[15]

As Douglas suggests, the women's magazine quiz—like the confession album before it, but unlike the detached "temperament analyses" of the AIFR—is an *intimate* form. It cultivates an air of sisterly closeness through its use of the second person, the way it addresses you directly and "invite[s] you to confess." But there is something deceptive, even sadistic, about the form, too: it is capable of turning your candor against you, or exploiting it to sell you things. A kind of promise is made to the reader, and then almost immediately betrayed. And this happens multiple times over, every month.

To take a psychological test is to put your trust in science (or pseudoscience, as the case may be). To take a quiz is to put your trust in an omniscient, benevolent magazine editor. Both of them involve a sort of quasi-religious faith. It's a type of faith based on familiarity, which can often shade into contempt without undermining the basis of the faith, and it has been essential to the development of passionate online fan bases for quizzes, personality tests, purity tests, and other questionnaire-based forms. Even if you don't share your answers with anyone, you've given up a part of yourself to a higher authority: you have confessed.

It's likely that the popularity of personality tests diminished their scientific standing—already quite low by the end of the 1960s, as we have seen—even further. But this very process of vulgarization has led to another turn of the screw that Galton began twisting back in 1870. It allowed questionnaires, freed from any requirement to be accurate, to be *fun*. This is another legacy of the *Cosmo* quiz: it transformed the marriage counseling questionnaire from something onerous into something onanistic, a guilty pleasure as opposed to a wifely duty. If personality tests had remained under the aegis of science, they would never have become beloved on the enormous scale they are today. Just as, in the Victorian era, women cajoled men into filling out confession albums, it took the adoption of the personality test by women's magazines—for many, especially many men, the epitome of abject, disposable popular culture—to make them palatable to everyone.

The consequences of this paradigm shift took decades to become clear, but forty-five years later, now that we are well into the Internet era, they are unmistakable. *Cosmopolitan* taught us—first women, and then men—to take quizzes compulsively, with a peculiar mixture of pleasure and anxiety. But in order to keep track of our answers, we needed something else: computers.

6 DATING AND DATA

Computer dating services probably have the highest response rates of any questionnaires in history. Ever since Galton's time, there has been a gulf between the questions that the writers of questionnaires wanted to ask and those that people wanted to answer. Those framing the queries have tended to be most interested in political opinions, consumer preferences, and medical or mental health: all topics the average citizen tends to consider private, dull, repellent, or all of the above. But when it came to love, all bets were off: no question was too personal, too prosaic, or too irrelevant.

If you were to add up the user bases of the leading dating websites Match.com, Chemistry.com, OkCupid, and eHarmony, you'd get a number in the tens of millions. All these sites use the questionnaire as the basic building block of their information architecture. Over the years, the software that sorts the data for computer dating services has grown immensely more sophisticated, able to weight variables and detect statistical patterns at a speed that would have made early computer scientists' heads spin. But the essential informational input has changed very little since the inception of computer dating in the 1950s. The proprietary algorithms of Match.com, eHarmony, OkCupid, and the rest are all fed on a steady diet of personal questions.

At the head of a long line of computer dating impresarios stands a familiar figure: Paul Popenoe. In the mid-1950s, at the apex of his fame as a marriage counselor, Popenoe collaborated with computer scientists at Remington Rand on the world's first computer dating program. The program seems to have been developed primarily as a publicity stunt to promote the UNIVAC, a powerful mainframe that had already been used to process census data and had accurately predicted the 1952 presidential election. (Gallup must have been quaking in his boots.) Popenoe was commissioned by Rand to write a thirty-two-item questionnaire to help match single men and women looking for committed, monogamous relationships. Questions included "Do you prefer double or twin beds?," "Do you like pets in the house?," and "Do you prefer smoking or drinking?"[1] The questionnaire was distributed to over 4,000 people; their answers were then coded on to punch cards and fed into the maw of the UNIVAC, which matched the most compatible respondents.

In November 1956, Popenoe appeared on Art Linkletter's television show *People Are Funny* in tandem with the UNIVAC computer itself to unveil their grand experiment to the world. "With a blinking of lights, a digestion of digits, and melodies played out on a monochromatic scale, the giant electronic brain took over TV last week," *Time* reported. The UNIVAC's initial matches ("John Caran, 28, a

Los Angeles adman, and pretty, brown-eyed Barbara Smith, 23, a receptionist") were introduced to one another for the first time live on air.[2] The show followed their courtship over the course of subsequent weeks, climaxing with the announcement of their engagement.

John and Barbara eventually called it off, but Linkletter kept trying. In later seasons, he even added a hypnotist to help UNIVAC-selected couples get in the mood. Eventually, the computer succeeded in matching Robert Kardell and Shirley Saunders, who married, to much media fanfare, in 1958. "It was love at first bleep," the *Gettysburg Times* reported.[3]

Once the technology was in place, computer dating caught on quickly. Two New York-based companies, Scientific Introduction Service and Project Technical Automated Compatibility Testing (TACT), were pioneers in the field. By the late 1960s, they were joined by a raft of competitors with names like Intramatics, Human Inventory, Date Mate, Select-A-Date, and Duo Date Processing.[4] In a 1966 feature story for *Look* magazine titled "boy . . . girl . . . computer," Gene Shalit reported on Operation Match, "the dig-it dating system that ties up college couples with magnetic tape" started by three Harvard students in 1965. In keeping with its collegiate origins and the changing times, Operation Match's questions were quite a bit more risqué than Popenoe's; items included "Is sexual activity [in] preparation for marriage, part of 'growing up'?" and "Do you believe in a God who answers prayer?"[5]

Still, there is more than a methodological relation between even the most libertine computer dating services and Popenoe's "positive eugenics." Of all the current major American dating sites, the one that hews closest to the Popenoeian philosophy is eHarmony, founded in the year 2000 by Neil Clark Warren, a Christian marriage counselor in Popenoe's adopted hometown of Pasadena. In its early years, it was affiliated with Focus on the Family's James Dobson, who got his start in the 1970s as one of Popenoe's assistants at the AIFR. Conservatism is baked right into eHarmony's user interface: the site automatically rejects users who report that they are currently married, have been married more than four times in the past (and are under 60), or who score low on its custom-made "dysthymia scale," indicating "severe depression."[6] The site matches only heterosexual couples, ostensibly because its research on human compatibility doesn't extend to gay culture. (In 2009, in response to a discrimination lawsuit, the company launched a same-sex dating site called Compatible Partners.)[7]

Other dating sites are less puritan in their mores but still fetishize their scientificity in ways that hearken back to Popenoe's heyday. Chemistry.com, for instance, was designed in collaboration with the anthropologist Helen Fisher, who, on the basis of fMRI brain scans as well as ethnographic research, claims that there are "four biologically-based personality types": "Explorer," "Builder," "Director," and "Negotiator." Which one you are depends on the precise combination of chemicals in your body: Explorers have a lot of dopamine, Builders a lot of serotonin, Directors a lot of testosterone, and Negotiators a lot of estrogen. Fisher's questionnaire, written with the psychologists Jonathan Rich and Heide Island, is designed to determine users' personality type and match them to a complementary partner, a process that involves a rather complex calculation of mutual desire: "Explorers are attracted to other Explorers. . . . Builders also gravitate to people like themselves, other Builders. Directors, however, gravitate to Negotiators. And Negotiators are drawn to Directors."[8] Where eHarmony sticks to basic vitae and the sort of "getting to know you" questions that would likely come up over the course of the first few dates anyway, Chemistry.com flaunts its esoteric knowledge of personality type. The first question you're asked, after you sign up, is "Which one of the following images most closely resembles your right hand?" Other visually oriented items include "If you are stuck in a boring meeting, or at an airport, what would your doodle look like?" and an opinion-scale question accompanying the statement "There is definitely something exciting on the other side of that wall."

All computer dating programs are built on a quasi-eugenic premise: that the fitness of a potential mate can be determined objectively, thus allowing "inappropriate" sexual partners to be screened out. Without subscribing to their racial theories, they share with Popenoe and Galton a belief that human qualities can be quantified and that, once this data is collected and correlated, a better social order can be engineered. On these sites, the sentimental romantic idea that "there is one special person out there for everybody" meets the hardheaded scientific belief in the precise measurement of everything. If everyone has a soul mate, why not use the superior processing power of a state-of-the-art algorithm to help discover that person?

*

The essential function of a dating site is to match couples based on informational input. But that is not all they do. The most successful sites spawn subcultures of their own, creating new social categories alongside those native to the dating pool. Chemistry.com encourages people to think of themselves as Negotiators or Builders, just as the MBTI encourages people to think of themselves as ENTJs. These are not just maps of the world of romance: for many people, they are part of the territory itself.

Furthermore, it is becoming increasingly clear that they do far more with their users' personal data than use it to set them up. A case in point is OkCupid. While it is far from the most successful dating site in raw numbers, OkCupid has had perhaps the greatest influence on the style of contemporary Internet culture at large. The company evolved from The Spark, a late 1990s startup that specialized in online study guides for high school and college students. Like Operation Match, The Spark was founded by a group of Harvard undergrads. Though they were running a real—and profitable—business from day one, the copy on The Spark's website, mostly written by creative director Christian Rudder, was satirical and playful in the manner of the *Harvard Lampoon* or *McSweeney's*. The 2001 version of The

Spark.com's "About Us" page, still accessible via the Internet Archive, reads like an absurdist parody of tech-sector corporate jargon. Under the heading "Pretty Good Privacy Policy," it says: "To ensure our users' security, we encrypt all data packets as rap songs." Under "Energizing Corporate Culture," it says: "Ours is a culture of violence. Beatings are frequent. Upward mobility is restricted to dung and tufts of hair. Wages are paid in pus. None thrive. None thrive. . . . Learning and growing aren't just gerunds at TheSpark.com, they're grounds for dismissal."

In addition to the study guides that were their bread and butter, The Spark.com featured tongue-in-cheek personality quizzes, modeled on the MBTI and the *samizdat* "purity tests" that had circulated for decades among adolescent and postadolescent nerds. Titles included "The Personality Test," "The Slut Test," "The Bastard Test," "The Ass Quiz," and "The Death Test." It also made two early stabs at computer dating programs, "Pimpin' Cupid" and "SparkMatch" ("founded on the idea that the Internet is the ideal medium for people to seize their own genitals and steer them towards each other").[9] Neither of these features quite caught on, but they laid the foundation for a future triumph: OkCupid, which the original Spark founders started in 2007. OkCupid retained the flippant style of The Spark but got more serious about data analytics; OkTrends, an entertaining numbers-crunching blog written by Rudder, was one of the site's most popular features. OkCupid featured staff-written personality quizzes similar to the ones that had been popular at The Spark, but it also encouraged users to add questions of their own, which were then answered by other users and analyzed by the site's algorithm to help make better matches.

There was an element of Barnumesque hucksterism to all this. "OK Cupid opened a parlor-game emporium and then got down to the business of pairing off the patrons," Nick Paumgarten wrote in a 2011 profile of the website's founders in the *New Yorker*. "The quizzes had no bearing on the matching. . . . They were merely bait—a pickup line, a push-up bra." But the line between quiz-as-bait and quiz-as-data is, in fact, not so clear-cut. One of the masterstrokes of OkCupid is that it's very difficult to separate the silly, throwaway questions from the statistically determinative ones. There is, apparently by design, a lot of noise among the signals on OkCupid. Unlike eHarmony, whose questionnaire is earnest and all-business, OkCupid will mix in seemingly trivial questions like "Do spelling mistakes annoy you?" and "Do you have a TV in your bedroom?" The natural impulse is to take these queries about as seriously as you would the Slut Test, but on OkCupid your answers to even the most ludicrous prompts have statistical consequences. Data is data, and when enough of it is compiled, patterns of *some* kind will inevitably emerge. As Paumgarten notes, "Some questions are unpredictably predictive"; for instance, "the answer to the question 'Do you like the taste of beer?' is more predictive than any other of whether you're willing to have sex on a first date."[10]

OkCupid tries harder than most dating sites to engineer a *casual* environment. When the general atmosphere is so loose and freewheeling, you feel more inclined to hang around the site and answer question after question. It feels less like a screening interview at a marriage clinic and more like small talk at a frat party, where every question might be prelude to a potential hook-up, or might mean nothing at all. After a while, answering questions begins to feel like an end in itself: not simply a necessary step on the way to finding a mate, but a way to kill time or amuse oneself in the moment.

OkCupid, then, may not be the best at matching couples who stay together and go on to have fulfilling relationships. But it *is* the best at getting its users to answer an enormous volume of personal questions—far more than even the most ambitious of midcentury social scientists would have dreamed. That raw data is used to match OkCupid's customers, but it's also sold (as Paumgarten reported in 2011) to academic social scientists, and probably to other outside parties as well. Finally, and most controversially, it's used by OkCupid itself to perform various experiments, analyses, and A/B trials, many of which have little to nothing to do with the company's core identity as a dating website.

In the last couple of years especially, OkCupid's promiscuous relationship with data has raised a host of ethical concerns. In July 2014, Rudder—still the de facto public face of the company, even though he is no longer involved in its daily operations—revived the long-dormant OkTrends blog to publish a post entitled "We Experiment on Human Beings!" In it, he described various experiments that OkCupid had conducted over the years: temporarily removing the pictures from user profiles, temporarily removing the profile text, and deliberately pairing couples with low matching scores. "We noticed recently that people didn't like it when Facebook 'experimented' with their news feed," Rudder wrote, referring to the online furor over the revelation of Facebook's attempts to manipulate its users' moods. "But guess what, everybody: if you use the Internet, you're the subject of hundreds of experiments at any given time, on every site. That's how websites work."

The chummy tone of Rudder's post ("Guess what, everybody") is disarming. Like all good rhetorical performances, it manipulates its audience on multiple levels, stoking the reader's paranoia with its supervillainish headline (that exclamation point!), and then almost immediately dispelling any sense of the sinister in its first paragraph: "OkCupid doesn't really know what it's doing," Rudder shrugs. "Neither does any other website. It's not like people have been building these things for very long, or you can go look up a blueprint or something. Most ideas are bad. Even good ideas could be better. Experiments are how you sort all this out."[11]

"We Experiment on Human Beings!," which raised the predictable hackles on social media and at left-leaning media outlets, was most likely a calculated provocation designed to build buzz for his book *Dataclysm: Who We Are (When We Think No One's Looking)*, published a couple of months later.

Rudder begins *Dataclysm* in an ironic register not far from that of The Spark's 2001 mission statement: "You have by now heard a lot about Big Data: the vast potential, the ominous consequences, the paradigm-destroying *new paradigm* it portends for mankind and its ever-loving websites." But in what follows, Rudder mostly dodges the question of whether tech companies are overreaching when it comes to collecting personal information, preferring to brag about the massive size of his own data set. "Instead of asking people survey questions or contriving small-scale experiments, which was how social science was done in the past, I could go and look at *what actually happens* when, say, 100,000 white men and 100,000 black women interact in private," he writes. "The data was sitting right there on our servers. It was an unprecedented sociological opportunity." He boasts that he has "probably put together a data set of person-to-person interaction that's deeper and more varied than anything held by any other private individual—spanning most, if not all, of the significant online data sources of our time"; it "encompasses thousands of times more people than a Gallup or Pew study."

Of course, none of the people represented in this data set agreed to be part of a study, nor did they sign the informed-consent agreements that are prerequisites for any legitimate research on human subjects in the social sciences. But Rudder makes it clear that his company's concern for its users' privacy has always been pretty much nil. Among other "experiments," he describes mining OkCupid's private message archive, remarking that "outside researchers rarely get to work with private messages like this—it's the most sensitive content users generate and even anonymized and aggregated message data is rarely allowed out of the holiest of holies in the database. But my unique position at OkCupid gives us special access." Nor does he attempt to hide the fact that the company profits from the sale of its users' personal data: "As a founder of an ad-supported site, I can confirm that data *is* useful for selling. Each page on a website can absorb a user's entire experience—everything he clicks, whatever he types, even how long he lingers—and from this it's not hard to form a clear picture of his appetites and how to sate them."

Dataclysm is an odd book, but it is one that is very much of our cultural moment: part self-congratulatory memoir by a millionaire entrepreneur, part work of amateur sociology with progressive political intentions. Rudder devotes many pages to arguing that racism is "systemic and pervasive" in American society, even among self-declared liberals: "It is no longer socially acceptable to be openly racist. . . . But it is still implicit in many of the decisions we make." (His statistical evidence for this includes the relative unpopularity of black women users on OkCupid, and the sudden spike in Google search results for the word "nigger" on the night of Barack Obama's election in February 2008.) He also notes, ambivalently, the extension of assessment and evaluation into almost every facet of online activity. "Tests like Myers-Briggs and Stanford-Binet have long been used by employers, schools, the military," he writes. "You sit down, you do your best, and they sort you. For the most part, you've opted in. But it's increasingly the case that you're taking these tests just by living your life."[12]

What's ultimately most significant about *Dataclysm* are not Rudder's findings—which neither unsettle common sense nor meet the standards of true scientific rigor—but the enormous information asymmetries they reflect. With OkCupid, Rudder and his colleagues have established what the technologist Jaron Lanier calls a "siren server": a powerful computer network with exclusive access to a specific type of data (in this case, answers to personal questions relating to dating preferences) and proprietary sorting algorithms to help make sense of it all. Mining all of this data helps OkCupid maximize its utility, which, in turn, helps reinforce the company's success in the marketplace. As Lanier points out, the most important thing for a "siren server" is to be first, or at least relatively early, on the scene, since strong "network effects" kick in once the server has compiled enough customer data to make itself into a useful resource, thus attracting further users.[13] The more people use OkCupid, the better the site gets: not simply because there is a larger pool of potential matches (that could actually be a negative, especially if many of the users are, by the site's standards, "undesirable"), but because there is more data for the algorithms to digest and learn from.

Leaving aside, for the moment, any ethical concerns about what tech companies like OkCupid decide to do with their users' personal information—an issue to which we will shortly return—we should note an odd by-product of this data-capture process. In the age of Big Data, answers to questionnaires that earlier generations of scientists like Bertram Forer and Walter Mischel would have tossed away as junk have become scientifically useful again, simply by virtue of being collected and analyzed at a much larger scale. While the basic input of an OkCupid answer may be less valid than your average psychometric test result, the fact that the site gets millions of people to answer hundreds of questions, and can easily connect their responses to basic vitae like age, gender, and geographical location, renders the data analytically valuable in a whole new way. As Rudder notes, the data set collected by sites like OkCupid "encompasses thousands of times more people" than even the most well-funded opinion survey. Given the scale at which questionnaires can be distributed and the speed with which they can be analyzed by algorithms backed up by the necessary processing power, it is relatively simple to home in on the results that *do* have some validity, find significant statistical correlations between them, and extract some kind of meaningful conclusion from the data set as a whole. In such a circumstance, the *quality* of the typical answer matters less than the *quantity* of total answers.

Accepting the kinds of experiments that companies like OkCupid routinely run on their users as "scientific" means abandoning the clinical paradigm of questionnaire research for a new data-driven paradigm. For midcentury scientists, the validity of the instrument and the accuracy of the result was of paramount importance; the inaccuracy of the final result was what made critiques like Forer's and Mischel's possible. But for soi-disant "data scientists" like Rudder, what matters most is having a lot of computational power and the ability to crunch an enormous set of numbers very quickly. If there are patterns, the computer will find them; the noise in the data set is no match for the siren server's ability to detect a signal. Many of the connections will be spurious, but the scale of the enterprise is such that some information of value will inevitably come to light.

This is a game that corporate executives are better positioned to play, and win, than academics. No surprise, then, that the rise of data science has unsettled the hierarchical relationship between accredited university scientists and big tech companies. If social scientists need to go to OkCupid or Facebook to get their data, their control over the quality of that data—and the potential political agendas toward which research can be oriented—plummets precipitously. The owners of siren servers hold all the cards. For the analyzers of questionnaires, it is the best of times and the worst of times: the holiest of holies is finally accessible, but there's a merchant guarding the gate.

7 QUIZ MANIA

I'm quite privileged. I should be a writer. I should live in Portland. I should go to Stanford. I belong in the 1980s. If I were a dog I'd be a Lab. If I were a billionaire tycoon I'd be George Soros. If I were a philosopher I'd be Karl Marx. If I were a punk icon I'd be Patti Smith. Like Saint Jude, I am fierce, kind, and cool as a cucumber. If I were an element I'd be carbon. If I were a character on *The Simpsons* I'd be the Inanimate Carbon Rod. If I were a font I'd be Futura. If I were a design aesthetic I would be the aesthetic void of a college dorm room. The food that best matches my personality is spaghetti and meatballs. My medieval profession would be a witch doctor. If I were a David Bowie I'd be Present Day Bowie. If I were a ghost I'd be an Orb.

What about you? If you've logged on to Facebook in the past two years, you almost certainly witnessed some similarly bizarre existential pronouncements, always accompanied by an invitation to discover and declare your own identity: "Which ___ Are You?" The majority of these quizzes are produced by BuzzFeed, a Manhattan-based company founded in 2006 by the new-media wunderkind Jonah

Peretti; though BuzzFeed has several rivals in the online quiz industry, it towers over the competition in both raw numbers and cultural influence.

The basic format of the typical BuzzFeed quiz is extremely simple. You are asked a series of questions, usually no more than nine or ten, each accompanied by a grid of multiple-choice answers illustrated with colorful images sourced from online image repositories like Photobucket or public message boards like Reddit. (A slight variation on the format allows for a checklist rather than a series of multiple-choice options.) Some of these quizzes deal with matters of concern to any adult human being with a modicum of autonomy over his or her life: "What City Should You Actually Live In?" "What Career Should You Actually Have?" Others cater to niche pop-cultural interests: "How Well Do You Know Your Muppets?" "Which Whit Stillman Character Are You?" Many touch on identity politics or, like *Cosmo*'s "Liberation" quizzes, profess a kind of consciousness-raising agenda: "How Privileged Are You?" "How Stereotypically White Are You?" Others are digital versions of carnival guessing games: "Can We Guess Your Age By Your Technology Preferences?" "Can We Guess Your Zodiac Sign Based on Your Favorite Body Shop Butter?" Some quizzes test knowledge, usually of pop culture; others are pegged to hard news or current events, though these attempts at timeliness are often in questionable taste (take a bow, "Which Ousted Arab Spring Ruler Are You?"). Quite a few quizzes are what BuzzFeed calls "branded content," meaning they are paid for by "BuzzFeed

Partners"—that is, advertisers—and designed to promote particular products: a "Which Expendable Are You?" quiz tied to the release of *The Expendables 3*, a "Which Barbie Doll Are You?" quiz underwritten by Mattel.

At this point it's a little hard to imagine subject matter that would seem surprising or inappropriate for a BuzzFeed quiz. Indeed, part of the allure of the quizzes stems from their omnivorousness, the way they manage to broach topics, from white supremacy to the "shady tweets" of Zayn Malik from One Direction, that might initially seem either too weighty or too trivial for the form to accommodate.

The most popular BuzzFeed quizzes are aspirational: they imagine a version of yourself more uniquely suited to your environment. As of December 2015, the all-time record-breakers are "What State Do You Actually Belong In?" (42,008,598 page views), "What City Should You Actually Live In?" (20,961,344), and "What Career Should You Actually Have?" (18,778,836). The use of the intensifying adverb "Actually" in all three of these titles registers a sense that the lives the quiz-takers are living are not the true ones. "Just because you were born somewhere doesn't mean you belong there," the brilliant subheadline to "What City Should You Actually Live In?" reads. The quizzes tell you less about who you are than what you should, or could, be. Geography is not destiny; the real is not the actual; "belonging" is a form of longing that may be satisfied by clicking a button and projecting yourself into the warmth of an imagined community. Taking these quizzes you feel, however obscurely, the excitements and satisfactions of lives you could be living, as well as the possibilities inherent in the answers you imagine *other* people providing.

At this point you may well want to object: No one takes these quizzes seriously! This is, broadly, true. BuzzFeed quizzes are explicitly presented as entertainments, not scientific instruments, and many of the people who post their quiz results to social media platforms like Facebook or Twitter preface them with some kind of light-hearted statement of disavowal: *I think this result is wrong, I think this is stupid, I can't believe I'm wasting my time on this fucking quiz when I should be working.*

Of course, from a business point of view, it doesn't matter whether we take BuzzFeed's quizzes seriously or not; what matters is that we take them, and we do. While the numbers have dropped off since the heady days of early 2014, when the combination of novelty and the viral lift from the Facebook algorithm allowed some posts to reach page view counts in the octuple digits, quizzes are still a consistent traffic driver for BuzzFeed. The site currently publishes as many as eighteen per day. As was the case with the Victorian confession album, BuzzFeed quizzes are treated sincerely by some and scornfully by others: to judge by my Facebook feed, at least, hatequizzing appears to be almost as popular a contemporary mode of consumption as hatewatching. But BuzzFeed gets the clicks whether you make fun of them or not, and they're laughing all the way to the next round of venture capital funding.

Quizzes are only one of many examples of BuzzFeed's knack for monetizing the zeitgeist. Jonah Peretti, the company's founder and CEO, has made a career out of exploring the intersection of technology, media, and capitalism. In the early 1990s Peretti attended the University of California at Santa Cruz, majoring in environmental studies and taking courses in the school's famously avant-garde History of Consciousness program. "I came out of a university system that was, at that particular moment in the '90s, glorifying postmodern critical theory," Peretti told the journalist Felix Salmon in 2014. "There was a sense that the best way to show you understand something is to write something incomprehensible."[1] In 1996, the year he graduated from Santa Cruz, Peretti published an (actually fairly comprehensible) article in the online journal *Negations* entitled "Capitalism and Schizophrenia: Contemporary Visual Culture and the Acceleration of Identity Formation/Dissolution." "My central contention is that late capitalism not only accelerates the flow of capital, but also accelerates the rate at which subjects assume identities," Peretti wrote. "Identity formation is inextricably linked to the urge to consume, and therefore the acceleration of capitalism necessitates an increase in the rate at which individuals assume and shed identities."[2]

Peretti's essay, which began as a term paper for one of his History of Consciousness classes, is rife with references to postmodern theorists like Deleuze and Guattari, Jameson, Butler, and Lacan. But his basic thesis is not far from the point

Susan Douglas makes about the way the women's magazine quizzes of the sixties and seventies "exaggerated [readers'] psychic schizophrenia." Asking questions can orient people in social space, but it can also disorient them. Some queries bolster a sense of identity and personal integrity (*I know the answer to this one; here's what I think*); others unsettle it (*I've never thought about that before; I'm not sure what to say*). What's new in Peretti's formulation, though, is his emphasis on the *acceleration* of this process. In 1996, he attributes this quickening of tempo, somewhat vaguely, to "late capitalism," but today we might be more tempted to pin it on the dizzying pace of social media and Internet publication. It's as if the college-age Peretti already foresaw the world he would help to define.

After Santa Cruz, Peretti went on to do graduate work at the MIT Media Lab, where he studied education and game design. At the same time, he dabbled in "culture jamming," planning and executing high-concept agitprop pranks under the aegis of a loose collective called the Contagious Media Project. In 2001 Peretti ordered a pair of customized Nike sneakers with the word "sweatshop" stitched on them; the company refused to fulfill the order, and Peretti's trolling e-mail exchange with a Nike customer service representative went viral after he forwarded it to ten friends. With his sister, the comedian Chelsea Peretti, he created a website called "Black People Love Us," which satirized the eagerness of white liberals to brag about their black friends. This, too, went viral.

These early stunts piqued Peretti's interest in the way content gets disseminated online, then a relatively new object of inquiry. But the anticapitalist emphasis of his earliest work didn't last long. Like George Gallup and Paul Lazarsfeld before him, Peretti was quickly recruited by advertisers and media executives who anticipated, perhaps before he did, the consequences of his work for their bottom line. Through the sociologist Duncan Watts, an acquaintance from the MIT Lab, he met the media executive Kenneth Lerer, who brought him on to help launch the Huffington Post in 2005. A year later, Peretti launched BuzzFeed. In 2007, he and Watts collaborated on an article for the *Harvard Business Review* entitled "Viral Marketing in the Real World." The techniques that Peretti had honed to critique capitalism were now being used to assist it.

Quizzes were not among BuzzFeed's most popular offerings at first. According to editorial director Summer Anne Burton, they only took off in 2013, when the site's Web development team began to focus on providing editors with "comprehensive quiz tools" and a cleaner, more attractive visual template. A June 2013 quiz called "Which 'Grease' Pink Lady Are You?" (subheadline: "There are worse things you could do than take this quiz") proved, unexpectedly, to be the site's most-shared piece of content at the end of the year. The corporate culture of BuzzFeed is strongly oriented toward replicating accidental successes, and after the *Grease* quiz's success Burton called an editorial staff meeting to discuss the potential for further quizzes. Soon millions of people were coming to the site specifically to take quizzes, and even contributing their own, using a platform called "BuzzFeed Community."[3]

The evolution of the BuzzFeed quiz recapitulates the history of questionnaires in miniature. Through trial and error, BuzzFeed's editors discovered that personality quizzes worked better than trivia challenges: BuzzFeed's readers seemed to prefer being told who they were to having their knowledge tested, just as Americans generally preferred psychological inventories like the MBTI to intelligence tests like the SAT. They also found that "identity-based" quizzes— keyed not only to racial and ethnic identities but also to online fandoms and neglected demographics—were reliably safe bets. This realization has resulted in micro-targeted quizzes like "What Kind of Goth Are You?"

The common denominator among these various underserved online subcultures is youth. BuzzFeed's content, as everyone knows, is particularly popular among "millennials": a nebulous concept, like all generational categories, but usually defined as encompassing everyone born between the early 1980s and the early 2000s. But "millennial" is not simply a handy term for the site's core demographic: it is also a consistently recurring theme of the quizzes themselves. Cultural reference points tend to center on the 1990s, when the oldest millennials were coming of age. Dewy nostalgia ("Which 'Fresh Prince of Bel Air' Character Are You?") sits easily beside expressions of hip contemporaneity ("Which Song from 'Empire' Describes

Your Life?") and state-of-the-art technology consumption ("Let Us Decide Whether You Should Buy the Apple Watch"). Quizzes like "Did You Actually Grow Up in the 90s?" and "Are You More of a 90s Kid or a 00s Kid?" do their best to demarcate these fuzzy borders, encouraging users to place themselves within the smallest generational box possible. This strategy shows no signs of flagging; Matthew Perpetua, BuzzFeed's Director of Quizzes and Games, told me in September 2015 that BuzzFeed's audience is "completely obsessed with age and generation."[4]

The fact that BuzzFeed's young readers enjoy taking quizzes about what marks them generationally is fortuitous, since a large part of the company's standing in the media industry, and its attractiveness to investors and advertisers, is the perception that it has a special relationship to "millennials." Quizzes allow BuzzFeed to test and refine those categories, in ways that resemble nothing so much as a marketing survey. But unlike the subjects of traditional surveys, who are typically cajoled into participating with financial incentives and other perks, people clamor to take BuzzFeed quizzes like "So How Big of a Millennial Stereotype Are You Really?" These quizzes provide a space, at last, where marketers' hunger to define a demographic segment meets individuals' desire to be defined.

*

From the anticapitalist point of view that Peretti himself espoused back in his culture-jamming youth, the overlap between BuzzFeed's content and the world of viral marketing is, at minimum, a little tacky. Still, when you set BuzzFeed quizzes next to all the noxious forms of content polluting the Internet today—gossipy blogs doxing private citizens; dashed-off, error-riddled news aggregations based on third- or fourth-hand reporting; racist and misogynist screeds laced with death and rape threats—it hardly seems worth getting worked up about. The word that comes to mind is "harmless." The quizzes are easy to condescend to but hard to hate, and in an era when the intensity of our hatred often seems to determine where we train our cultural attention, they have mostly slipped under the outrage radar.

Nevertheless, some serious concerns have been raised about BuzzFeed's current quiz regime and its relation to the status quo of online data collection in general. One of these worries has been prominently, if not widely, expressed in the media: this is the possibility that BuzzFeed is collecting and selling quiz answer data to advertisers or marketers. In March 2014, in a story for NPR's *Marketplace*, the reporter Stacy Vanek Smith speculated that the answers to quizzes could be used as market research for the various corporations that partner with BuzzFeed. Describing a branded quiz sponsored by HBO called "How Would You Die in *Game of Thrones*?," Smith said "not only does HBO now know I watch *Game of Thrones*, in taking the quiz, I gave them a lot of information. My preferred alcohol: white wine. My last meal: a steak. My biggest fear: failure. My idea of heaven: A tropical beach. That is hugely valuable information."[5]

Thus far, BuzzFeed has denied that it's selling the user data generated by quizzes, or even collecting it beyond basic metrics like how many people have taken the quiz, whether they share it, and their final results.[6] But the claim that the company isn't recording detailed information about its users is demonstrably false. "When you visit BuzzFeed, they record *lots* of information about you," a June 2014 blog post by Dan Barker entitled "BuzzFeed is Watching You" begins. "Most websites record *some* information. BuzzFeed record a whole ton." As soon as you land on any BuzzFeed page, Barker notes, custom variations to the site's Google Analytics code allow it to see whether you've arrived via Facebook, your age, gender, the country you're currently in, and how many times you've shared BuzzFeed content in the past. In the particular cases of quizzes, the site also records each "event" (i.e., each click on the page). "If you click 'I have never had an eating disorder'" (an actual checklist item from the "How Privileged Are You?" quiz) "they record that click," Barker writes.[7] This means that, in theory at least, BuzzFeed is in possession of some extraordinarily sensitive information about their users. Barker points out that BuzzFeed could easily generate a list of users who have had eating disorders, changed their gender, or taken medication for their mental health. From a marketing perspective, such data may be just as valuable as the fact that you eat steak or like white wine; from a privacy standpoint, of course, it is much more insidious.

Furthermore, there is already a lucrative market for this kind of personal information. Brokerage companies like Experian, BlueKai, and eXelate act as middlemen between publishers and social media platforms that collect user data, on the one hand, and advertisers and other potential purchasers of that data, on the other. Brokers stockpile this data, hosting it on their servers and analyzing it algorithmically in order to break it down into salable demographic segments. "Theoretically you could take all the people who are Darth Vader and should live in Seattle and who love Hello Kitty and, doing a little bit of analytics, you could discover that that segment is very likely looking for a new car," Aram Sinnreich, a communication scholar and expert on online privacy, told me.[8] (Just as with OkCupid, the triviality of the raw data doesn't mean that statistically significant correlations can't be drawn from it.) That segment could then be sold, in turn, to automobile companies looking to serve ads or offer discounts to only that tiny slice of users who visit *Star Wars* and Hello Kitty fan sites and have searched for plane fares to Seattle-Tacoma airport.

It should be said that there is no direct evidence that BuzzFeed is currently selling any of its users' personal data to third parties. What *is* clear, however, is that they have both the technological capability and a strong economic incentive to do so. Even if the answers to quizzes aren't currently being traded or shared, there's nothing to prevent BuzzFeed from collecting them now and selling them off at some later date, if their fortunes take a dip or they're bought by a larger company. As of this writing, there are very few legal restrictions on any of these practices, unless they involve medical information or children under the age of thirteen.

The lack of legal regulation of online data collection is striking, especially given how essential it has become to the media and advertising industries in recent years. These practices, critics argue, could have significant social consequences. In his 2011 book *The Daily You: How the New Advertising Industry is Defining Your Identity and Your Worth*, Joseph Turow anticipates a new form of class stratification arising from the fact that "marketers divide people into *targets* and *waste*"—that is, attractive and unattractive, from a marketing perspective—based on their digital data profiles. "Wide-ranging data points indicating the social backgrounds, locations, activities, and social relationships of hundreds of millions of individuals are becoming the fundamental coins of exchange in the online world," he claims. Once individuals have been sorted and categorized as either "targets" or "waste" based on analysis of their browsing and search histories as well as, quite possibly, their answers to online quizzes and questionnaires, the advertising messages they encounter online will be very different. "Those considered waste are ignored or shunted to other products the marketers deem more relevant to their tastes and income," Turow writes, while "targets are further evaluated in the light of the information that companies store and trade about their demographic profiles, beliefs, and lifestyles. The targets receive different messages and possibly discounts depending on those profiles."

The damage these practices do to equality of economic opportunity, and the potential for predatory or discriminatory pricing, is obvious. But there could well be political repercussions to these categorizations as well as economic ones. When you combine the data industry's division of the audience into "targets" and "waste" with the trend toward content personalization or "optimization"—in which not only the advertising but the actual content of a webpage changes, depending on the viewer's "reputation"—you begin to grasp how this kind of customized content could lend itself to social and political manipulation.[9] What if a "target" (whether, in a given instance, this means a wealthy person, a millennial, a white person, or a man) sees one version of a news story—one construction of reality—while a "waste" sees another? Could a corporation pay to suppress a given story for an entire income bracket, generational demographic, or geographical region? What would such unequal access to information mean for the shaping of public opinion? Could Super PACs pay to influence the coverage different types of people see during an election season? What about a personality test like Adorno's F-scale; couldn't it be used by political candidates to identify people likely to be receptive to their ideology, who can then be fed messages that reinforce it?

In *The Daily You*, Turow emphasizes the danger latent in the fact that few Internet users understand the full extent of online tracking, or the commercial uses to which their personal data can be put. "A comparison to the financial industry is apt," he writes. "Here was an industry engaged in a whole spectrum of arcane practices that were not at all transparent to consumers or regulators but that had serious negative impact on our lives. It would be deeply unfortunate if the advertising system followed the same trajectory."[10] It may be that, as in the case of finance, government regulation of the data industry is the answer—or one answer—to these dilemmas. In December 2013, Turow testified as an expert witness at a US Senate hearing on the subject convened by Senator John D. Rockefeller IV. In his introduction to the proceedings, Senator Rockefeller estimated that the data broker industry generated $156 billion in revenue in 2012 alone—"more than twice the size of the entire intelligence budget of the United States Government"—and yet, unlike "government or law enforcement agencies [that] collect information about us . . . data brokers go about their business with little or no oversight." Rockefeller said he was "disturbed by the evidence showing that data brokers segment Americans into categories based on their incomes, and they sort economically vulnerable consumers into groups with names like 'Rural and Barely Making It,' 'Tough Start: Young Single Parents,' 'Rough Retirement: Small Town and Rural Seniors,' and 'Zero Mobility.'"[11] Were these targeting practices to become more widely known, it's not hard to imagine a broad-based populist reaction against data brokers, on the order of the (temporary) outrage against bankers and derivative traders after the financial crash of 2008.

It's certainly possible that the coming years will see tougher state regulation of the data industry. One thing that's already clear, however, is that any such regulation will be staunchly opposed by the data brokers themselves. Tony Hadley and Jerry Cerasale, senior vice presidents of Government Affairs and Public Policy at Experian and the Direct Marketing Association, respectively, both testified at the 2013 hearing about the deleterious effects that regulation would have on the American economy. Hadley went so far as to call "the manner in which U.S. companies collect and share consumer information . . . the 'secret ingredient' to our productivity, innovation and ability to compete in the global marketplace."[12] The business model of companies like Experian is built on the invasion of users' privacy and the free exchange of their information among corporations, bringing to mind nothing so much as Adam Smith's observation that "people of the same trade seldom meet together . . . but the conversation ends in a conspiracy against the public."

Harder to predict is where publishers like BuzzFeed, social media platforms like Facebook, and dating sites like OkCupid will come down on these issues. Is the collection and sale of user data enough of a priority for these companies for them to oppose government regulation? Would the sacrifice of public goodwill, if users come to believe that BuzzFeed, say, was exploiting the data gleaned from quizzes, offset the loss of profit generated by that exploitation?

No one knows for certain, but it's not too early to venture a guess. Almost all of the indicators—BuzzFeed's unprecedented level of comfort with branded content, Peretti's resistance to the idea of employee unionization[13]—

suggest a conspicuously business-friendly attitude on the part of the company, which is widely acknowledged to be at the vanguard of digital media. When the inevitable public fight over data, advertising, and the media begins, BuzzFeed will lead and others will follow, and it's hard to imagine the example they set will be a pro-regulatory one.

All of this concerns consumption: the things we buy or read or see, and our right of access to them. But mass data collection affects production, too: the way we work, and the means by which that work is managed. Already there are signs that BuzzFeed, and other tech companies like it, are ushering us back to an era like the one William H. Whyte described in the 1950s, in which questionnaires and tests are used to make hiring decisions and monitor workplace performance.

Paradoxically, BuzzFeed itself may not be the best place to see this happening. In media circles, the company is well known for providing a relatively pleasant, even cushy work environment. They are awash in venture capital funding and seem to be constantly hiring. The staff is unusually racially diverse, and despite Peretti's public opposition to unionization, by all accounts he is a liberal and open-minded boss who places a strong emphasis on experimentation and employee autonomy, and that laissez-faire attitude filters down through the rest of the company. On the face of it, nothing could be further from the Taylorized, tested workplace dystopia Whyte described at midcentury.

What may end up being most significant from a labor perspective, however, is not the environment at BuzzFeed itself but the changes that it might make possible at other workplaces. From the beginning, Peretti's vision of BuzzFeed has been linked to a specific set of white-collar labor conditions, and a very particular vision of how the world of work is structured. Way back in 2006, while still working at the Huffington Post, Peretti posted an online manifesto based around a sketchy idea called the "Bored at Work Network." "Hundreds of millions of bored office workers sit in front of computers forwarding emails, blogging, IMing, and playing on social network sites," Peretti wrote. "These distracted corporate employees have accidentally created the Bored at Work Network (BWN)—a huge people-powered network with even greater reach than traditional networks like CNN, ABC, or the BBC."[14] It was this audience—white-collar employees who are at work but not, for the moment, actually working—that BuzzFeed was originally designed to service. Its content, notwithstanding the occasional healthful serving of long-form journalism or cultural criticism, is still largely made up of bite-size nuggets that can be consumed quickly between tasks, or during stolen moments when your boss isn't looking.

This strange convergence of the work environment and the media environment is now so ordinary, for so many people, that we rarely even think about it at all. But it is unprecedented. Historically, Americans have not read news articles, watched videos, or played games while at work. (The occasional crossword puzzle under the desk, maybe.) Not only would these activities have been difficult to disguise from superiors, in a way that surreptitiously clicking from one tab to another on a computer is not: it would just not have occurred to anyone to try to do these things in the workplace. Nor would they have spent their stolen moments answering questions about themselves. Questionnaires, as Whyte's *The Organization Man* reminds us, were associated with management, and with control: they were, for the most part, resented, feared, and despised.

But BuzzFeed, like OkCupid before it, has engineered a virtual environment in which people actively *enjoy* answering questions about themselves. The stakes feel vanishingly low; the questions, and answers, are amusing; the ability to immediately share the results with friends, often in a spirit of mock triumph or indignation, adds an irresistible exhibitionistic element. For a lot of us, fucking around and taking quizzes on websites like BuzzFeed is now *part* of the labor process, as routinized as bathroom or cigarette breaks; and this is true whether we work in offices or in Internet-enabled cafes or from our homes.

In the mid-1950s, American white-collar workers took personality tests when they were forced to by their superiors; six decades later, we take and retake them, voluntarily, almost every single day of our lives. This shift in the way we work—or, more precisely, the way we procrastinate—is happening in tandem with the development of new technologies that track employee behaviors in previously unimaginable detail. In "They're Watching You at Work," a 2013 feature story for the *Atlantic*, Don Peck reported that personality testing, which had fallen into disrepute since its high point in the early 1960s for legal as well as scientific reasons, is making a comeback in human resources departments. He described "app-based video games . . . designed by a team of neuroscientists, psychologists, and data scientists" for the purpose of assessing job candidates; twenty minutes' worth of play was enough to "generate several megabytes of data, exponentially more than what's collected by the SAT or a personality test." A company named Evolv produces "tests [that] allow companies to capture data about everybody who applies for work, and everybody who gets hired—a complete data set from which sample bias, long a major vexation for industrial-organization psychologists, simply disappears." In the near future, as language analysis technology improves, Peck anticipates "programs that [will] automatically trawl through the e-mail traffic of [the] workforce, looking for phrases or communication patterns that can be statistically associated with various measures of success or failure in particular roles." But already the amount of knowledge that sophisticated managers can extract from their employees' "data signatures" is enormous: "Torrents of data are routinely collected by American companies and now sit on corporate servers, or in the cloud, awaiting analysis," Peck writes.[15]

Let's imagine that all of the trends Peck describes continue to accelerate, uncurbed by government regulation or populist backlash. Now imagine that what these perpetually surveilled white-collar workers habitually do, when they're bored, is visit BuzzFeed and take a quiz. The information they provide about themselves will probably seem trivial, ephemeral, and unrelated to whatever it is they do for work. (It may also, of course, be totally inaccurate.) Nonetheless, there is nothing preventing the quiz publisher from logging this data and selling it—perhaps with a detour through a third-party data broker like eXelate, Experian, or BlueKai—back to the bored workers' employers.

What could businesses do with this data, once they have it? If it's properly anonymized, they will be unable to use it to punish or reward individual employees, which, for those who fear the social Internet becoming a capitalist panopticon, is some kind of comfort at least. But they will still be able to employ it to rationalize changes in hiring, management, or corporate strategy. It could be used to justify targeted layoffs: not by ratting out individual underachievers (again, assuming the data was kept anonymous) but by constructing types and categories of "desirable" and "undesirable" workers. Peck reports that high-level computer programming skills are strongly correlated with visits to a particular Japanese manga site. If such unexpected correlations are already being used to identify exceptional job candidates, what's to stop companies from taking the next step and using them to filter out "undesirable" ones?

The politics of Big Data are still up for grabs, though it's difficult to believe that things won't ultimately tilt in the direction of management rather than labor. Bosses will probably prefer pouring money into data analytics—just as they once did into personality tests—to raising wages. There may be lip service paid, as there was in Isabel Myers's time, to employee morale and "fitting the worker to the job," but the bottom line will be efficiency. Some companies may eschew this kind of optimization for ethical reasons, or because of public disapproval, or because they don't realize its benefits. Others will be priced out of the competition: only the richest will be able to play the game of data to win.

There is, for that matter, no reason why the sort of recreational data provision that BuzzFeed is encouraging in our culture couldn't be pressed into the service of something still worse: a revival of eugenics, perhaps, provided the data could be correlated with details on race, ethnicity, or country of origin. Modern-day nativists like Donald Trump (who has publicly endorsed the idea of creating a database of Muslims living in the United States) might well sign on to versions of the agendas advanced by eugenicists like Robert Yerkes and Carl Brigham.[16] It is true that, for the time being, the ideologies espoused by data barons like Peretti, Christian Rudder, and Mark Zuckerberg are (antiunionism aside) fairly progressive. They want to use the awesome capabilities of their proprietary platforms to advance science, expose racism, and promote the free exchange of ideas that is vital to an open society. They want—in a formulation that is by now a Silicon Valley cliché—to make the world a better place. But so did Galton, and Gallup, and Popenoe, and nearly everyone else who, over the course of the past century and a half, has tried to devise new ways to get people to answer questions about themselves, or new purposes to put the answers to. It has not always worked out so well.

The art of asking questions is as liable to misuse as any other art. Information on what people are like, and what they enjoy, think, or believe, is one of the most powerful props supporting any official ideology. Gallup recognized this back in 1940: it's why he insisted that accuracy in the gauging of public opinion was a crucial part of what separated democracy from dictatorship. Today, the psychological line separating serious inquiries from casual probes has been all but wiped out, while the technological power to collect, sort, and deploy the data that result from these researches grows to gargantuan proportions.

"Here is the voice of The Organization," Whyte wrote in 1956, of workplace personality tests, "and if one wishes to judge what the future would be like were we to intensify organization trends now so evident, let him ponder well what the questions are really driving at."[17] Today Whyte's paranoid style can seem a bit overblown: there is no monolithic Organization, just a tangled network of small-o organizations with shifting, temporarily aligning interests.

Nevertheless, let us ponder: Where is all this headed? What are the new questions driving at?

Think before you answer. This is not a test.

ACKNOWLEDGMENTS

Many people have helped me immeasurably in the production of this book. David Auerbach, Summer Anne Burton, Ashley Perez, Matthew Perpetua, Doree Shafrir, Aram Sinnreich, and Stacy Vanek Smith all generously agreed to interviews. Russell Brandom, Tim Carmody, Kristiania Clark, Lori Cole, Kevin Driscoll, Merve Emre, Suzanne Fischer, Mary Kim, Leila A. McNeill, Joanna Neborsky, Matt Pearce, and various members of the Writers' Room Slack cabal shared advice, ideas, leads, and work in progress. Colin Dickey, Rob Horning, Hua Hsu, Claire Jarvis, Joshua Joy Kamensky, Ariana Kelly, Phil Maciak, Ben Merriman, Sarah Mesle, Rebecca Onion, Nikil Saval, Jennifer Schnepf, Jacqui Shine, Moira Weigel, and Ben Wurgaft read and commented on individual chapters and provided invaluable feedback. David Yourdon took on the Herculean labor of reading a first draft of the entire manuscript with only a week until the deadline. Hundreds of friends, acquaintances, and even some total strangers kept me sane by providing support, encouragement, suggestions, and comic relief across various social media platforms.

Particular thanks go to Amina Cain and Ariana Kelly, who invited me to deliver the talk from which the idea for this book originally sprang at their Errata Salon lecture series in Los Angeles. Ted Scheinman did terrific work editing a version of Chapter 3 for *Pacific Standard*. Ian Bogost and Christopher Schaberg provided intelligent criticism and sage guidance. Haaris Naqvi encouraged this project from a very early stage, and ably shepherded it into print. Alice Marwick designed a gorgeous cover that made me more excited to finish a book to go along with it. Kathy Daneman came up with ingenious stratagems for getting it in front of people.

Thanks, affection, and admiration go to my parents Jeffrey and Louise Kindley, who have probably influenced the contents of this book in ways I can't begin to understand. And thanks, most of all, to Emily Ryan Lerner: my wife, my best friend, my rock and foundation.

NOTES

Introduction

1 "2015 Match Fact Sheet," accessed November 21, 2015, "What State Do You Actually Belong In," accessed November 21, 2015, http://www.buzzfeed.com/awesomer/what-state-do-you-actually-belong-in.

2 Adam Fox, "Printed Questionnaires, Research Networks, and the Discovery of the British Isles, 1690–1800," *The Historical Journal* 53, no. 3 (2010): 593–621.

3 Lisa Gitelman, *Paper Knowledge: Toward a Media History of Documents* (Durham, NC: Duke University Press, 2014).

Chapter 1

1 Francis Galton, *Memories of My Life* (New York: E. P. Dutton & Company, 1909), 291–93.

2 Francis Galton, *English Men of Science: Their Nature and Nurture* (London: Macmillan & Co., 1874), 263–66.

3 Galton, *English Men of Science*, 127.

4 Francis Galton, "Eugenics: Its Definition, Scope, and Aims," accessed November 21, 2015, http://www.mugu.com/galton/

essays/1900-1911/galton-1904-am-journ-soc-eugenics-scope-aims.htm.

5 D. W. Forrest, *Francis Galton: The Life and Work of a Victorian Genius* (New York: Taplinger, 1974), 136; Nicholas Wright Gillham, *A Life of Sir Francis Galton* (New York: Oxford University Press, 2001), 196.

6 Quoted in Gillham, *A Life of Sir Francis Galton*, 342.

7 Francis Galton, "Medical Family Registers," *Fortnightly Review* 40, no. 34 (August 1883): 244–47.

8 Samantha Matthews, "Psychological Crystal Palace: Late Victorian Confession Albums," *Book History* 3 (2000): 125–54.

9 Aubrey Beardsley, "The Story of a Confession Album," accessed November 21, 2015, http://www.cypherpress.com/beardsley/juvenilia/confession.asp.

10 Fabrice Touttavoult, *Confessions: Marx, Engels, Proust, Mallarmé, Cezanne* (Paris: Belin, 1988), 62.

11 Berge's remarks are quoted in Henry-Jean Servat, "A Question of Proust," *The Proust Questionnaire* (Costa Mesa, CA: Assouline, 2005).

12 "Proust Questionnaire Sells for $120,000," *TheAdvocate.com*, May 28, 2003, accessed November 21, 2015, http://www.advocate.com/news/2003/05/28/proust-questionnaire-sells-120000-8764.

13 Quoted in Graydon Carter, "The Proustian Bargain," *VanityFair.com*, October 31, 2009, accessed November 21, 2015, http://www.vanityfair.com/culture/2009/11/proust-book-200911.

14 Sadly, the Turbo Proust feature seems to have disappeared as of November 28, 2015, http://www.vanityfair.com/culture/2009/10/proust-questionnaire.

15 James Lipton, *Inside Inside* (New York: Dutton, 2007), 453.

16 Marcel Proust, *Marcel Proust on Art and Literature*, trans. Sylvia Townsend Warner (New York: Carroll & Graf, 1997), 99–104.

Chapter 2

1 Robert M. Yerkes, ed., *Psychological Examining in the United States Army* (Washington, DC: United States Surgeon-General's Office, 1921), 208, 282, accessed November 21, 2015, https://archive.org/details/psychologicalexa00yerkuoft.

2 Carl C. Brigham, *A Study of American Intelligence* (Princeton, NJ: Princeton University Press, 1923), vii–viii, 177, accessed November 21, 2015, https://archive.org/details/studyofamericani00briguoft.

3 Quoted in Stephen Jay Gould, *The Mismeasure of Man* (New York: W. W. Norton & Company, 1996), 254–55.

4 Woodworth Psychoneurotic Inventory, accessed June 4, 2015, http://personality-testing.info/tests/WPI.php.

5 Quoted in Michael M. Sokal, "James McKeen Cattell and American Psychology in the 1920s," in *Explorations of the History of Psychology in the United States*, ed. Joseph Brožek (Lewisburg, PA: Bucknell University Press, 1984), 287.

6 Michael Zickar, "Using Personality Inventories to Identify Thugs and Agitators: Applied Psychology's Contribution to the War against Labor," *Journal of Vocational Behavior* 59 (2001): 159.

7 William H. Whyte, *The Organization Man* (Philadelphia: University of Pennslvania Press, 2002), 38, 179, 405.

8 Martin L. Gross, *The Brain Watchers* (New York: Random House, 1962), 10.

9 Annie Murphy Paul, *The Cult of Personality: How Personality Tests Are Leading Us to Miseducate Our Children, Mismanage Our Companies, and Misunderstand Ourselves* (New York: Free Press, 2004), 59.

10 Quoted in Graham Richards, *Race, Racism, and Psychology: Towards a Reflexive History* (London: Routledge, 2012), 105.

11 Bertram Forer, "The Fallacy of Personal Validation: A Classroom Demonstration of Gullibility," *Journal of Abnormal and Social Psychology* 44 (1949): 118–23.

12 Ross Stagner, "The Gullibility of Personnel Managers," *Personnel Psychology* 11, no. 3 (September 1958): 347–51.

13 Walter Mischel, "Looking for Personality," in *A Century of Psychology as Science*, ed. Sigmund Koch and David E. Leary (Washington, DC: American Psychological Association, 1985), 517–23.

Chapter 3

1 Carl G. Jung, "Introduction to *Psychological Types*," in *The Essential Jung*, ed. Anthony Storr (Princeton, NJ: Princeton University Press), 129–33.

2 Katharine Cook Briggs, "Meet Yourself: How to Use the Personality Paint Box," *The New Republic* (December 22, 1926): 129–32.

3 Frances Wright Saunders, *Katherine and Isabel: Mother's Light, Daughter's Journey* (Boston: Nicholas Brealey, 1995), 109.

4 Paul, *The Cult of Personality*, 112.

5 John H. Wolfe, "Personality Testing in the Church of Scientology: Implications for Outcome Research," 2–3, accessed November 21, 2015, http://cogprints.org/9080/1/Scientology_OCA2.pdf.

6 Quoted in Chris Owen, "The Fallacy of the Oxford Capacity Analysis (OCA)," accessed June 5, 2015, http://www.solitarytrees.net/cowen/misc/am2oca.htm.

7 "Oxford Capacity Analysis," accessed June 4, 2015. http://www.xenu.net/archive/oca/.

8 John Foster, *Enquiry into the Practice and Effects of Scientology* (1971), accessed May 20, 2015, http://www.xenu.net/archive/audit/foster05.html.

9 Quoted in Chris Owen, "The Fallacy of the Oxford Capacity Analysis (OCA)."

10 "Scientology Blamed in High-Profile Suicide," *UPI.com* (April 16, 2008), accessed November 21, 2015, http://www.upi.com/Top_News/2008/04/16/Scientology-blamed-in-high-profile-suicide/UPI-71481208365208/.

Chapter 4

1 George Gallup and Saul Forbes Rae, *The Pulse of Democracy: The Public-Opinion Poll and How It Works* (New York: Simon & Schuster, 1940), v; the book was coauthored by Saul Rae, a colleague of Gallup's at the American Institute of Public Opinion, but for ease of reference—and because the ideas expressed in the book were popularly associated with Gallup's name alone—I have credited Gallup as the sole author in the main text.

2 Robert Wuthnow, *Inventing American Religion: Polls, Surveys, and the Tenuous Quest for a Nation's Faith* (Oxford: Oxford University Press, 2015), 15–24.

3 Gallup and Rae, *The Pulse of Democracy*, 7, 10.

4 Quoted in B. Z. Doktorov, *George Gallup: Biography and Destiny* (Moscow, 2011), accessed November 21, 2015, http://romir.ru/GGallup_en.pdf.

5 Statistics taken from https://www.math.upenn.edu/~deturck/m170/wk4/lecture/case1.html (the *Literary Digest*'s prediction and sample sizes) and http://www.presidency.ucsb.edu/data/ (Gallup's prediction and the final tally), accessed November 21, 2015.

6 Gallup and Rae, *The Pulse of Democracy*, 71–2.

7 Ibid., 56.

8 Ibid., 64, 68.

9 George Gallup, "The Quintamensional Plan of Question Design," *The Public Opinion Quarterly* 11, 3no. (Autumn 1947): 385–93.

10 Paul F. Lazarsfeld, "The Art of Asking Why in Marketing Research: Three Principles Underlying the Formulation of Questionnaires," *National Marketing Review* 1 (1935): 26–38.

11 Paul F. Lazarsfeld, "An Episode in the History of Social Research: A Memoir," in *The Varied Sociology of Paul F. Lazarsfeld*, ed. Patricia L. Kendall (New York: Columbia University Press, 1982), 21.

12 Herbert H. Hyman, *Taking Society's Measure: A Personal History of Survey Research* (New York: Russell Sage Foundation, 1991), 194.

13 Lazarsfeld, "An Episode in the History of Social Research: A Memoir," 17–19, 58.

14 Theodor W. Adorno, "Scientific Experiences of a European Scholar in America," in *The Intellectual Migration: Europe and*

America: 1930–1960, ed. Donald Fleming and Bernard Ballyn (Cambridge, MA: Harvard University Press, 1969), 338–70.

15   T. W. Adorno, Else-Frenkel Frenkel-Brunswik, Daniel J. Levinson, and R. Nevitt Sanford, *The Authoritarian Personality* (New York: Harper and Brothers, 1950), 4, 13, 24, 226–27.

Chapter 5

1   "George Gallup: Some Answers from the Question Man," *St. Petersburg Times* (April 23, 1976), D1.

2   "Cheerios, the 'Terribly Adult Cereal,'" accessed November 24, 2015, https://www.youtube.com/watch?v=PauDwNFPucU.

3   Jill Lepore, "Fixed," *The New Yorker* (March 29, 2010), accessed November 30, 2015, http://www.newyorker.com/magazine/2010/03/29/fixed.

4   Molly Ladd-Taylor, "Eugenics, Sterilisation and Modern Marriage in the USA: The Strange Career of Paul Popenoe," *Gender & History* 13, no. 2 (August 2001): 300.

5   Alexandra Minna Stern, *Eugenic Nation: Faults & Frontiers of Better Breeding in Modern America* (Berkeley, CA: University of California Press, 2005), 150–51, 167, 178.

6   *Ironwood Daily Globe* (October 2, 1934), 3.

7   Reprinted in *Women's Magazines 1940–1960: Gender Roles and the Popular Press*, ed. Nancy A. Walker (London: Palgrave Macmillan, 1998), 125.

8   Ladd-Taylor, "Eugenics, Sterilisation and Modern Marriage in the USA," 310.

9   Joan Didion, "Marriage à la Mode," reprinted in *Women's Magazines 1940–1960: Gender Roles and the Popular Press*, 258–59.

10 Sarah Laskow, "In search of the ur-quiz." *Columbia Journalism Review* (March 17, 2014), accessed November 21, 2015, http://www.cjr.org/behind_the_news/in_search_of_the_ur-quiz.php.

11 Barbara Creaturo and Veronica Geng, eds, *Cosmopolitan's Hangup Handbook* (New York: Cosmopolitan Books, 1971), xxi, 299.

12 Susan Brownmiller, *In Our Time: Memoir of a Revolution* (New York: The Dial Press, 1999), 85–86.

13 Jennifer Scanlon, *Bad Girls Go Everywhere: The Life of Helen Gurley Brown* (Oxford: Oxford University Press, 2009), 180.

14 Creaturo and Geng, *Cosmopolitan's Hangup Handbook*, 265.

15 Susan J. Douglas, *Where the Girls Are: Growing Up Female with the Mass Media* (New York: Three Rivers Press, 1995), 100.

Chapter 6

1 "Univac Plays Cupid Role; Couple Will Get Married," *Pampa Daily News* (November 18, 1956), 14.

2 "Radio: Electronic Cupid," *Time* (November 19, 1956), accessed November 29, 2015, http://content.time.com/time/magazine/article/0,9171,867279,00.html.

3 "UNIVAC Played Cupid in 1st Mating by Automation," *Gettysburg Times* (October 16, 1958), 1.

4 "Loneliness Game Turns into Multi-Million Dollar Business," *Lincoln Star Sun* (January 22, 1967), 32.

5 Gene Shalit, "boy . . . girl . . . computer . . .", *Look* (February 22, 1966): 30–35.

6 "They Met Online, But They Definitely Didn't Click," *Washington Post* (Mar 13, 2007), D01.

7   "eHarmony Launches Gay Dating Site," *Christianity Today* (March 31, 2009), accessed November 21, 2015, http://www. christianitytoday.com/women/2009/march/eharmony-launches-gay-dating-site.html; http://www.christiantoday. com.au/article/eharmony.launches.gay.dating.site/5982.htm.

8   Helen Fisher, *Why Him? Why Her?: Finding Real Love by Understanding Your Personality Type* (New York: Henry Holt, 2009), 7–11.

9   The Spark home page, as it would have appeared in 2001. Accessed via the Internet Archive on August 24, 2015.

10   Nick Paumgarten, "Looking for Someone," *The New Yorker* (July 4, 2011).

11   Christian Rudder, "We Experiment on Human Beings!", OkTrends blog, accessed November 21, 2015, http://blog. okcupid.com/index.php/we-experiment-on-human-beings/.

12   Christian Rudder, *Dataclysm: Who We Are (When We Think No One's Looking)* (New York: Crown, 2014).

13   Jaron Lanier, *Who Owns the Future?* (New York: Simon & Schuster, 2013).

Chapter 7

1   Felix Salmon, "BuzzFeed's Jonah Peretti Goes Long," *Matter* (June 11, 2014), accessed November 21, 2015, https:// medium.com/matter/buzzfeeds-jonah-peretti-goes-long-e98cf13160e7.

2   Jonah Peretti, "Capitalism and Schizophrenia: Contemporary Visual Culture and the Acceleration of Identity Formulation/ Dissolution," *Negations* (1996), accessed November 21, 2015,

http://www.datawranglers.com/negations/issues/96w/96w_peretti.html.

3   Interview with Summer Anne Burton, conducted by author, June 23, 2014.

4   Interview with Matthew Perpetua, conducted by author, September 4, 2015.

5   Stacy Vanek Smith, "Quizzes are free data mining tools for brands," *Marketplace* (March 18, 2014), accessed November 21, 2015,. http://www.marketplace.org/2014/03/18/business/quizzes-are-free-data-mining-tools-brands.

6   Kara Bloomgarden-Smoke, "BuzzFeed Isn't Selling Your Data From All Those Quizzes," *Observer.com* (March 21, 2014), accessed November 29, 2015, http://observer.com/2014/03/buzzfeed-could-monetize-your-data-from-all-those-quizzes/.

7   Dan Barker, "BuzzFeed is Watching You," *barker.co.uk*, accessed November 21, 2015, http://barker.co.uk/buzzfeediswatching.

8   Interview with Aram Sinnreich conducted by author, May 28, 2014.

9   Joseph Turow, *The Daily You: How the New Advertising Industry is Defining Your Identity and Your Worth* (New Haven, CT: Yale University Press, 2011), 88–89, 122–25.

10 Turow, *The Daily You*, 8.

11 "What Information Do Data Brokers Have on Consumers, and How Do They Use It?" (December 18, 2013), accessed November 18, 2015, http://www.commerce.senate.gov/public/index.cfm/2013/12/what-information-do-data-brokers-have-on-consumers-and-how-do-they-use-it.

12 Testimony of Tony Hadley, "What Information Do Data Brokers Have on Consumers, and How Do They Use It?,"

accessed November 21, 2015, http://www.commerce.senate.
gov/public/_cache/files/41e8b66d-0273-43fa-b7ad-35502ca
ce722/2FEACC87D15F8DD0065905570808DB8F.hadley-
testimony.pdf.

13 Hamilton Nolan, "Jonah Peretti is Not Your Friend," *Gawker*
(August 17, 2015), accessed November 21, 2015, http://gawker.
com/jonah-peretti-is-not-your-friend-1724519279.

14 Accessed August 24, 2015, http://www.contagiousmedia.
org/. As of December 2015, the official Contagious Media
Project page is no longer online, though the text of the BWN
manifesto is still archived on various other sites.

15 Don Peck, "They're Watching You at Work," *The Atlantic*
(December 2013), accessed November 21, 2015, http://www.
theatlantic.com/magazine/archive/2013/12/theyre-watching-
you-at-work/354681/.

16 Jenna Johnson, "Donald Trump would 'certainly' and
'absolutely' create a database of Muslims," *Washington Post*
(November 20, 2015), accessed November 29, 2015, https://
www.washingtonpost.com/news/post-politics/wp/2015/11/20/
donald-trump-would-certainly-and-absolutely-create-a-
database-of-muslims/.

17 Whyte, *The Organization Man*, 179.

INDEX